Poison Ivy

This weed (above) causes an itchy rash if you touch it. Poison ivy grows as a vine or shrub. Try to remember what the leaves look like, and do not touch them or other parts of the plant. If you do touch poison ivy, washing your hands as soon as possible may reduce the itching. Your local drugstore will have various remedies that will help.

Parts of an Insect

All insects have the following things in common:

1 An outside skeleton (or exoskeleton)
2 Three pairs of jointed legs
3 A body divided into three sections: head, thorax, and abdomen
4 External mouthparts on their head

World Book's

SCIENCE & NATURE GUIDES

INSECTS

OF THE UNITED STATES AND CANADA

World Book, Inc.
a Scott Fetzer company
Chicago

Scientific names

In this book, after the common name of an organism (life form) is given, that organism's scientific name usually appears. Scientific names are put into a special type of lettering, called italic, *which looks like this.*

The first name in a scientific name is the genus. A genus consists of very similar groups, but the members of these different groups usually cannot breed with one another. The second name given is the species. Every known organism belongs to a particular species. Members of the same species can breed with one another, and the young grow up to look very much like their parents.

An animal's scientific name is the same worldwide. This helps scientists and students to know which animal is being discussed, since the animal may have many different common names.

Therefore, when you see a name like *Limothrips cerealium*, you know that the genus is *Limothrips* and the species is *cerealium*. *Limothrips cerealium* is the scientific name for the grain thrip (see page 11).

Insect-hunter's Code

1 **Always go collecting with a friend**, and always tell an adult where you are going.

2 **Leave insects' nests** untouched.

3 **Treat all insects with care**—most are delicate creatures and can easily be injured or killed by handling. It always is best to observe only.

4 **Ask permission** before exploring or crossing private property.

5 **Keep to existing roads, trails, and pathways** wherever possible.

6 **Keep out of crops and leave fence gates** as you find them.

7 **Ask permission** before exploring or crossing private property.

8 **Wear long pants, shoes, a hat, and a long-sleeved shirt** in tick country.

This edition published in the United States of America by World Book, Inc., Chicago.

WORLD BOOK and the GLOBE DEVICE are registered trademarks or trademarks of World Book, Inc.

World Book, Inc.
233 North Michigan Avenue
Chicago, IL 60601 USA

For information about other World Book publications, visit our Web site **http://www.worldbook.com,** or call **1-800-WORLDBK (967-5325).** For information about sales to schools and libraries, call **1-800-975-3250 (United States); 1-800-837-5365 (Canada).**

Copyright © 2005 Chrysalis Children's Book Group, an imprint of Chrysalis Books Group Plc
The Chrysalis Building, Bramley Road, London, W10 6SP
www.chrysalis.com

Library of Congress Cataloging-in-Publication Data

Insects of the United States and Canada.
   p. cm. – (World Book's science & nature guides)
   Includes bibliographical references (p.).
   ISBN 0-7166-4214-X — ISBN 0-7166-4208-5 (set)
   1. Insects—North America—Juvenile literature. 2. Insects—North America—Identification—Juvenile literature. I. World Book, Inc. II. Series.

   QL473 .I55 2005
   595.7'097—dc22
                         2004041967

Text and captions based on *Insects of the Northern Hemisphere* by George C. McGavin. Species illustrations by Richard Lewington; habitat paintings by Philip Weare of Lindon Artists; headbands by Antonia Phillips; and identification and activities illustrations by Mr. Gay Galsworthy.

For World Book:
General Managing Editor: Paul A. Kobasa
Editorial: Shawn Brennan, Maureen Liebenson, Christine Sullivan
Research: Madolynn Cronk, Lynn Durbin, Cheryl Graham,
   Karen McCormack, Loranne Shields, Hilary Zawidowski
Librarian: Jon Fjortoft
Permissions: Janet Peterson
Graphics and Design: Sandra Dyrlund, Anne Fritzinger
Indexing: Aamir Burki, David Pofelski
Pre-press and Manufacturing: Carma Fazio, Steve Hueppchen,
   Jared Svoboda, Madelyn Underwood
Text Processing: Curley Hunter, Gwendolyn Johnson
Proofreading: Anne Dillon

Printed in China
1 2 3 4 5 6 7 8 9 10 09 08 07 06 05 04

Contents

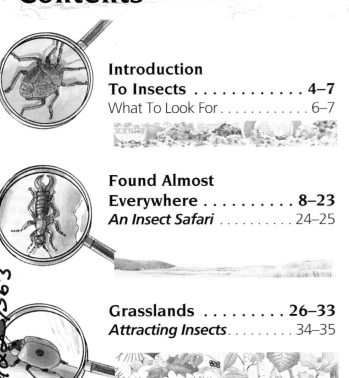

Entries **like this**
indicate pages
featuring
projects you
can do.

Introduction to Insects

Scientists have classified and named over 1½ million species, or kinds, of animals. About 1,000,000 of them are insects. Because there are so many different kinds of insects, this book describes only common families of insects. Typical species are identified in the pictures and often highlighted in the text.

Insects are invertebrates, which means that they do not have internal backbones as fish or snakes or dogs do. The first insects developed at least 400 million years ago—long before the dinosaurs!

Most insects have wings, which give them a great advantage over most other kinds of animals. With wings, insects can travel long distances to colonize new habitats, and they can escape from their enemies. Some insects can beat their wings up to 1,000 times per second.

From egg to insect

Insects are divided into groups, called orders. The most advanced insect orders, like Coleoptera or Lepidoptera, have a very complicated life cycle during which they change their shape three times. Each time, they look completely different from their previous shape. How this works is shown in the picture. The fly life cycle can be as short as 14 days or as long as several weeks or even months.

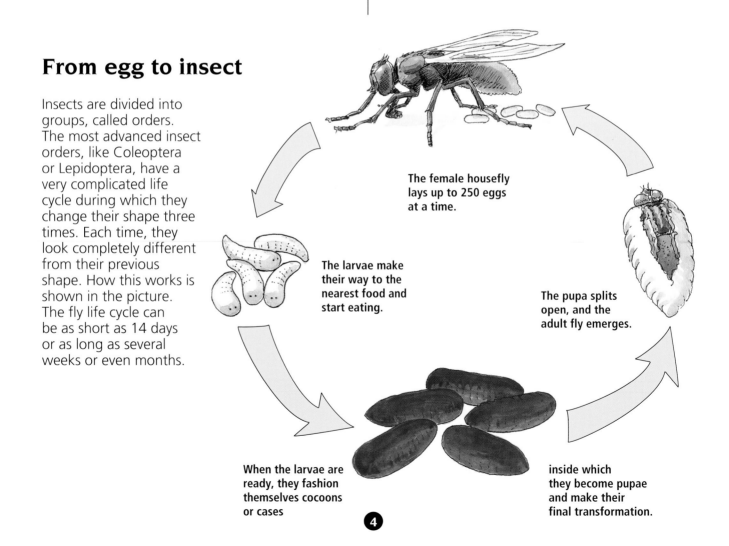

The female housefly lays up to 250 eggs at a time.

The larvae make their way to the nearest food and start eating.

When the larvae are ready, they fashion themselves cocoons or cases

inside which they become pupae and make their final transformation.

The pupa splits open, and the adult fly emerges.

Orders of insects

Insects belong to the phylum Arthropoda. The phylum is divided into several classes. Insects make up the class Insecta. The class is divided into orders according to insects' varying characteristics. Scientists believe there are many more species to be discovered. The largest orders are:

COLEOPTERA
Beetles
(about 350,000)

LEPIDOPTERA
Butterflies & Moths
(about 165,000)

HYMENOPTERA
Sawflies, Bees,
Wasps, & Ants
(about 120,000)

HEMIPTERA
Bugs, Cicadas, Scale
Insects, & Aphids
(about 90,000)

ORTHOPTERA
Grasshoppers
& Crickets
(about 20,000)

DIPTERA
True Flies
(about 119,500)

Top-of-page Picture Bands

Each section has a different picture band at the top of the page. These bands are shown below:

 **Found Almost Everywhere**

 **Grasslands**

 **Woods & Forests**

 **Deserts & Savannas**

 **Rivers & Wetlands**

 **Pests & Parasites**

How to use this book

This book will introduce you to the more common families of insects. Each family has an entry and a picture of a typical insect from the family. When trying to identify the insect you have found, expect it to look something like the picture, but not exactly the same. To identify an insect, follow these steps.

1 **Look at the list of the most common orders and their pictures** shown here. Which does the insect you are trying to identify most resemble? The identification chart on pages 6 to 7 will help you narrow down the options.

2 **Decide what habitat (environment) you are in.** If you aren't sure, read the descriptions at the start of each section to see which one fits best. Each section has a different picture band heading. These are shown at the left.

3 **Look through the pages of insects with this picture band.** The picture and information given for each insect family will help you to identify it. The large winged insect (below) is a sphinx moth (see page 23).

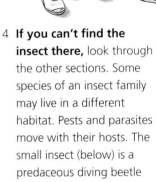

4 **If you can't find the insect there,** look through the other sections. Some species of an insect family may live in a different habitat. Pests and parasites move with their hosts. The small insect (below) is a predaceous diving beetle (see page 63).

5 **If you still can't find the insect,** you may have to look in a large field guide. You might have spotted something very rare or even unknown!

What To Look For

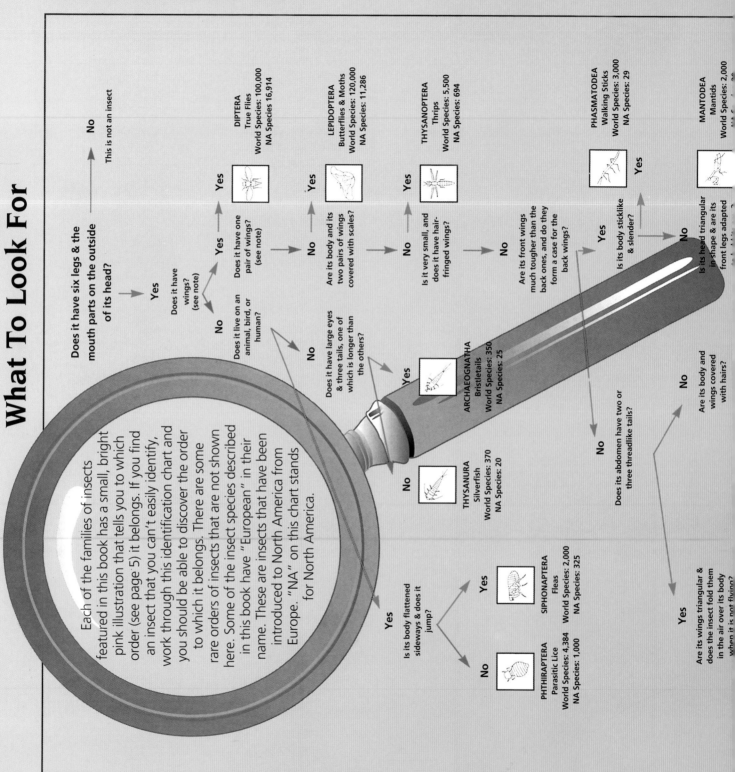

Each of the families of insects featured in this book has a small, bright pink illustration that tells you to which order (see page 5) it belongs. If you find an insect that you can't easily identify, work through this identification chart and you should be able to discover the order to which it belongs. There are some rare orders of insects that are not shown here. Some of the insect species described in this book have "European" in their name. These are insects that have been introduced to North America from Europe. "NA" on this chart stands for North America.

Does it have six legs & the mouth parts on the outside of its head?

No → This is not an insect

Yes

Does it have wings? (see note)

No ← → Yes

Does it have one pair of wings? (see note)

Yes

DIPTERA
True Flies
World Species: 100,000
NA Species: 16,914

No →

Are its body and its two pairs of wings covered with scales?

Yes

LEPIDOPTERA
Butterflies & Moths
World Species: 120,000
NA Species: 11,286

No →

Is it very small, and does it have hair-fringed wings?

Yes

THYSANOPTERA
Thrips
World Species: 5,500
NA Species: 694

No

Are its front wings much tougher than the back ones, and do they form a case for the back wings?

Yes

Is its body sticklike & slender?

Yes

PHASMATODEA
Walking Sticks
World Species: 3,000
NA Species: 29

No →

Is its head triangular in shape & are its front legs adapted

MANTODEA
Mantids
World Species: 2,000

Does it live on an animal, bird, or human?

No

Does it have large eyes & three tails, one of which is longer than the others?

Yes

ARCHAEOGNATHA
Bristletails
World Species: 350
NA Species: 25

No

THYSANURA
Silverfish
World Species: 370
NA Species: 20

Does its abdomen have two or three threadlike tails?

No

Are its body and wings covered with hairs?

Yes

Yes

Is its body flattened sideways & does it jump?

Yes

SIPHONAPTERA
Fleas
World Species: 2,000
NA Species: 325

No

PHTHIRAPTERA
Parasitic Lice
World Species: 4,384
NA Species: 1,000

Are its wings triangular & does the insect fold them in the air over its body when it is not flying?

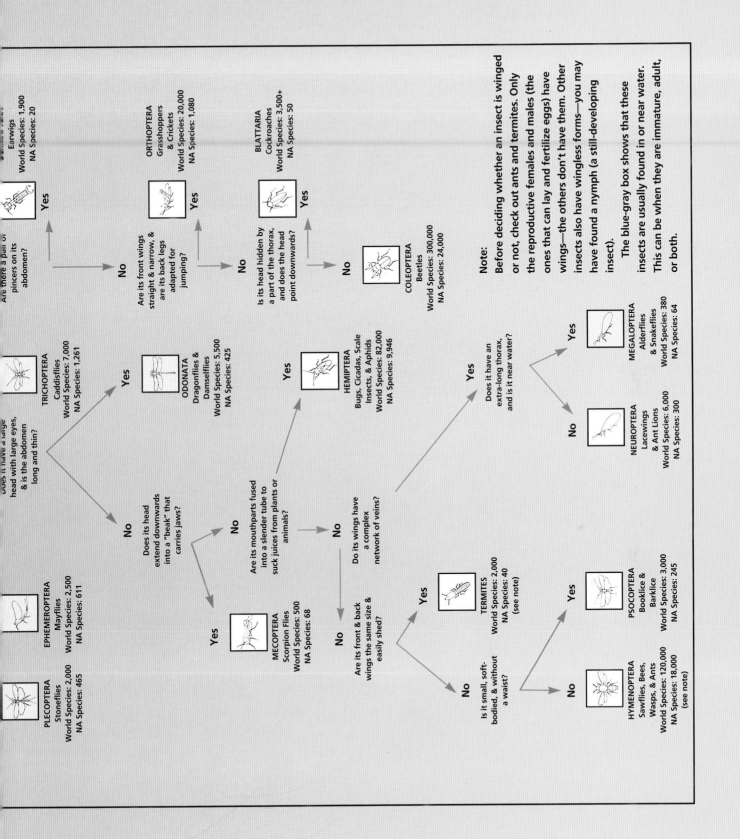

PLECOPTERA
Stoneflies
World Species: 2,000
NA Species: 465

EPHEMEROPTERA
Mayflies
World Species: 2,500
NA Species: 611

Does it have a large head with large eyes, & is the abdomen long and thin?

Earwigs
World Species: 1,900
NA Species: 20

Are there a pair of pincers on its abdomen?

Yes

TRICHOPTERA
Caddisflies
World Species: 7,000
NA Species: 1,261

Yes

ORTHOPTERA
Grasshoppers
& Crickets
World Species: 20,000
NA Species: 1,080

No

Are its front wings straight & narrow, & are its back legs adapted for jumping?

Yes

No

Yes

ODONATA
Dragonflies &
Damselflies
World Species: 5,500
NA Species: 425

BLATTARIA
Cockroaches
World Species: 3,500+
NA Species: 50

No

Does its head extend downwards into a "beak" that carries jaws?

No

Is its head hidden by a part of the thorax, and does the head point downwards?

Yes

No

Are its mouthparts fused into a slender tube to suck juices from plants or animals?

Yes

HEMIPTERA
Bugs, Cicadas, Scale
Insects, & Aphids
World Species: 82,000
NA Species: 9,946

COLEOPTERA
Beetles
World Species: 300,000
NA Species: 24,000

Yes

MECOPTERA
Scorpion Flies
World Species: 500
NA Species: 68

No

Do its wings have a complex network of veins?

No

Does it have an extra-long thorax, and is it near water?

Yes

MEGALOPTERA
Alderflies
& Snakeflies
World Species: 380
NA Species: 64

Yes

TERMITES
World Species: 2,000
NA Species: 40
(see note)

No

Are its front & back wings the same size & easily shed?

No

Yes

No

NEUROPTERA
Lacewings
& Ant Lions
World Species: 6,000
NA Species: 300

Is it small, soft-bodied, & without a waist?

No

PSOCOPTERA
Booklice &
Barklice
World Species: 3,000
NA Species: 245

Yes

HYMENOPTERA
Sawflies, Bees,
Wasps, & Ants
World Species: 120,000
NA Species: 18,000
(see note)

Note:
Before deciding whether an insect is winged or not, check out ants and termites. Only the reproductive females and males (the ones that can lay and fertilize eggs) have wings—the others don't have them. Other insects also have wingless forms—you may have found a nymph (a still-developing insect).

The blue-gray box shows that these insects are usually found in or near water. This can be when they are immature, adult, or both.

Found Almost Everywhere

The insect families described on the following pages are either very common or truly widespread. Many of them you will easily find in parks and yards, but many you may see anywhere from a city street to a seaside beach— and many places in between!

Yards and parks are a very important habitat for wildlife. Different vegetation provides habitat for a lot of different insects, many of whom often eat from only one type of plant. Large numbers of insects encourage more insectivores, like birds and shrews, to live in the area.

An average-sized, urban yard (measuring about 2,000 square feet [186 square meters]) with many shrubs, trees, and other plants may hold 200 to 300 different beetle species, up to 200 species of flies, and hundreds of bee and wasp species. In addition, there may be 80 to 90 bug species, and more than 300 species of butterflies and moths (mostly moths). Of course, many of those insects may be simply passing through.

This picture shows 13 kinds of insects from this section. How many can you identify?

Garden ant, alfalfa leafcutting bee, assassin bug, stink bug, painted lady butterfly, humpbacked fly, white-lined sphinx moth, hover fly, green lacewing, European corn borer, garden tiger moth, German yellow jacket, grain weevil

Cockroaches

Many of these large, fast-running cockroaches are brown or reddish-brown with a shiny appearance. Their oval, flattened bodies let them hide in narrow crevices. Their legs are bristled. When running about, they continually wave their antennae. They are found both in the wild and in buildings. A female American cockroach (*Periplaneta americana*, shown here) may lay up to 50 egg cases containing 12 to 14 eggs. Some species emit a foul-smelling liquid.

Order: Blattaria
Family: Blattidae
U.S. & Canada species: 6
World species: 3,500
Body length: 1/10–2⅓ in (0.25–5.8 cm)

Jumping Bristletails

If you search under stones in grassy areas or woods, in rock or leaf litter, or on rocks on the seashore above the high-tide line, you should find some of these little bristletails. You may find a leach (*Petrobius maritimus*, shown here) running over rocks and harbor walls close to the sea. These insects look a lot like silverfish (see page 74), but are brownish in color with a humped thorax. If you disturb them, they jump before running for cover. They feed mainly on algae, mosses, lichens, and decaying organic debris.

Order: Archaeognatha
Family: Machilidae
U.S. & Canada species: 14
World species: 250
Body length: Up to ½ in (1.3 cm)

Common Earwigs

Species in this family are found in ground litter, soil, under loose bark, or in rocky crevices. If you search in such places, you will soon find them—often dozens of individuals clustered together. In some species the female stands guard over her eggs. This is an example of primitive maternal care. She even licks the eggs to keep them free of infection. The pincers at the tail-end are used for courtship and defense. Despite their name, they are very unlikely to get into human ears. Some species are garden pests because they chew flower petals. The most common species, the European earwig (*Forficula auricularia*, shown here), was introduced to the United States from Europe in the early 1900's.

Order: Dermaptera
Family: Forficulidae
U.S. & Canada species: 20
World species: 465
Body length: ¼–1 in (0.6–2.5 cm)

Tube-tailed Thrips

Members of this family are found in small habitats such as herbaceous plants, shrubs, trees, flowers, twigs, and under bark. Some dwell in leaf litter and soil. Although this family contains some of the world's largest thrips, most are less than 1/25 inch (1 millimeter) long. While the majority feed on fungal threads and the spores of fungi, some are carnivorous.

Order: Thysanoptera
Family: Phlaeothripidae
U.S. & Canada species: 348
World species: 2,700
Body length: Up to 1/25 in (1 mm)

Haplothrips kurdjumovi

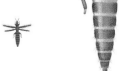

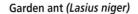

Ants

You can find ants in almost every color from pale yellow to black. They live in colonies and are adapted for their particular tasks. You will mostly see the

Garden ant (Lasius niger)

wingless workers, but the queens, who lay the eggs, and the males, who fertilize them, have wings. Look for ants disappearing into holes in the ground in your yard. They also live in natural cavities and build nests aboveground. Search in conifer woods for the great mounds of leaves and pine needles that are the home of wood ants. Ants can be herbivores or carnivores, or mixed feeders (omnivores). Many feed on the honeydew produced by aphids (see page 16) or the sap of plants. Some ants have powerful biting jaws. Others can sting you or spray formic acid, which stings.

Order: Hymenoptera—Family: Formicidae—
U.S. & Canada species: 696
World species: 10,000
Body length: ½₅–1 in (1 mm–2.5 cm)

Common Thrips

Common thrips are tiny. If you look carefully among flowerheads, peas, beans, and in the ears of grains, you should find plenty of specimens. Despite their small size, they are serious pests because they transmit virus diseases to many commercial crops. Sometimes these small insects are called thunderflies because they seem to fly around just before thunderstorms.

Order: Thysanoptera
Family: Thripidae
U.S. & Canada species: 264
World species: 1,500
Body length: up to ½₅ in (1 mm)

The grain thrip (Limothrips cerealium) is a pest that breeds in the ears of cereal crops. It is less than ⅛ inch (0.3 centimeters) long.

Green Lacewings

Green lacewings are very common, and you should easily be able to find some. They sometimes come to lighted windows and are mainly nocturnal. You will find them in all types of vegetation, where their prey—aphids, scale insects, and mites—live. Some species have incredible bat-detecting, ultrasonic sound receivers in the veins of their wings—a useful way to avoid being captured by a hungry bat. Green lacewings often hibernate in houses and attics.

Order: Neuroptera
Family: Chrysopidae
U.S. & Canada
species: 87
World species: 1,600
Body length: ¼–1 in
(0.6–2.5 cm)

The green lacewing (Chrysopa carnea) has bright golden, brassy, or reddish eyes, which seem to shine.

True Crickets

These are found in all kinds of woodlands, scrub, meadows, and grasslands. Most species hide under stones, logs, or leaf litter. Others live in trees, while some live underground, but certain members of this family will enter houses. Some are active by day, others by night. The species shown is the house cricket (Acheta domesticus), which was once very common in old houses and bakeries. It has been introduced to North America from Europe. Today, because of increased cleanliness and modern building methods, they are not found as often in these places.

Order: Orthoptera
Family: Gryllidae
U.S. & Canada species: 96
World species: 1,800
Body length: ½–¾ in (1–1.8 cm)

Burying or Sexton Beetles

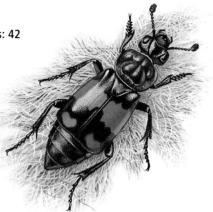

Order: Coleoptera
Family: Silphidae
U.S. & Canada species: 42
World species: 250
Body length:
1–1½ in (2.5–3.8 cm)

These beetles have a very sensitive sense of smell and are attracted to the dead bodies of small animals. The sexton beetle (*Nicrophorus vespilloides,* shown here), is a good example of the family. The adult beetles are very strong and two can move an animal as big as a rat. Their purpose in doing this is for the female to lay eggs on or near the carcass so that the larvae have a plentiful food supply. These beetles are very important in nutrient recycling and carcass disposal and are some of the most efficient refuse collectors of the insect world.

Ground Beetles

These beetles have well-developed legs and powerful jaws. They live in a wide range of habitats under stones, wood, and debris. If you lift such objects, you may see a ground beetle running away very fast. They catch and eat a large variety of invertebrates and carrion (dead and decaying flesh), although a few species feed on plants. Their larvae are also active hunters and live in soil and leaf litter. They have powerful jaws and use enzymes to dissolve their prey's insides. The adults of some species climb into trees and shrubs to catch and eat caterpillars.

Order: Coleoptera
Family: Carabidae
U.S. & Canada species: 2,271
World species: 20,000+
Body length: ⅟₁₆–3¼ in
(0.15–8.2 cm)

**Ground beetle
(*Calosoma
sycophanta*)**

Rove Beetles

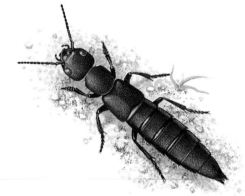

This family has very many species. Most are quite small and can run fast. Small species fly by day, while larger ones fly at night. This is a family of predators, scavengers, or herbivores. By searching under stones you may find a devil's coach-horse (*Staphylinus olens,* shown here). Three hundred species of rove beetles are associated with ants. They mimic their hosts and will offer them a sweet fluid to avoid attack. But they prey on injured or dead ants.

Order: Coleoptera—Family: Staphylinidae
U.S. & Canada species: 3,187—World species: 20,000+
Body length: ⅟₂₅–¾ in (1 mm–2 cm)

Sap Beetles

These beetles are often found on daisies. The adults feed on sap oozing from tree wounds, on flower nectar, decaying fruits, carrion, and other rotting matter. Some species are associated with ants and bees. People who wear yellow clothes in the summer may find they attract members of this family. They can ruin picnics and also seem to be attracted to bright, fresh paint. A few species prey on scale insects, and some feed inside plant seed pods.

Order: Coleoptera
Family: Nitidulidae
U.S. & Canada
species: 183
World species: 2,800
Body length: 1/16–1/2 in
(0.15–1.3 cm)

Pollen beetle
(*Meligethes aeneus*)

Leaf Beetles

Members of this family are found on every plant species and in all land habitats. The adults chew flowers and foliage. Their larvae feed in the same way, but also mine and bore through leaves, stems, and roots. Many of these smooth, rounded, and often shiny or colorful beetles are serious pests. Shown below is the notorious Colorado potato beetle (*Leptinotarsa decemlineata*). This species attacks potatoes, tomatoes, and eggplants. Some leaf beetle species can be useful in controlling weeds.

Order: Coleoptera
Family: Chrysomelidae
U.S. & Canada species: 1,481
World species: 25,000
Body length:
1/16–3/4 in (0.5–2 cm)

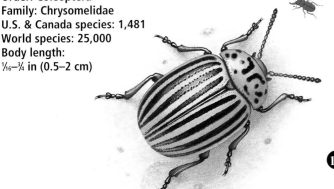

Weevils or Snout Beetles

The species of this gigantic family are by far the most common insects on Earth. All weevils have a snout or "rostrum" that carries the jaws. The family has members that feed on almost every species of plant. Nearly all are herbivorous and they eat every bit of a plant, from root to seed. If disturbed, a weevil usually lies quite still, or else folds its legs beneath its body and simply falls to the ground as if dead. Many species, like the grain weevil (*Sitophillus granarius*, shown here), are serious pests. The boll weevil is the major pest species that attacks the American cotton crop.

Order: Coleoptera
Family: Curculionidae
U.S. & Canada species: 2,700
World species: 40,000+
Body length: 1/16–1 1/2 in
(0.15–3.8 cm)

Checkered Beetles

Most members of this family have soft, slightly flattened bodies that are very hairy. The insects' coloring can be bright blue, green, red, dark brown, or pink. Checkered beetles can be found on the leaves of woody plants and in woody areas. The larvae prey on the larvae of bark beetles and other bark-boring beetles. Some others prey on the larvae of bees and wasps, and on grasshopper egg pods. Some species are able to find their prey by the pheromes (scents) they produce. The redlegged ham beetle (*Necrobia rufipes*, shown here) can damage stored meat and meat products.

Order: Coleoptera
Family: Cleridae
U.S. & Canada species: 266
World species: 3,500
Body length: 1/16–1 in
(0.15–2.5 cm)

Dance Flies

The common name of this predacious family comes from the mating swarms that occur in summer in which males fly up and down in a dancing fashion. They feed by catching small flies. Males sometimes offer prey items to females to eat while they mate with them. Some dance flies take prey from spiders' webs. Their habitat is moist places near water. Their larvae live in humus, leaf litter, decaying wood and vegetation, under bark, and in water. They eat black flies, scale insects, and mites. Much remains to be discovered about these insects.

Order: Diptera—Family: Empididae—U.S. & Canada species: 678 World species: 3,500—Body length: 1/16–1/2 in (0.15–1.3 cm)

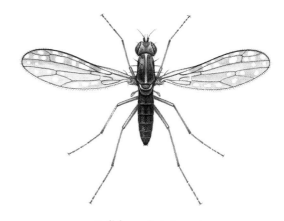

Dolichocephala irrorata

Blow Flies

Typical species of this family are the familiar bluebottle and greenbottle flies. They have metallic green or blue, shiny black, or dull coloration. In some species, the sexes are of different colors. You have most probably seen these flies attracted to your food. Adults also feed on flower pollen and nectar, as well as rotting animal and plant matter. Being fond of carrion and dung makes them carriers of diseases such as dysentery. A very unpleasant species lays its eggs on the wool of sheep. The larvae then bore into the flesh of the sheep, leaving terrible wounds. Other species attack worms, and still others suck the blood of nesting birds.

**Order: Diptera
Family: Calliphoridae
U.S. & Canada species: 78
World species: 1,200
Body length: 1/8–1/2 in
(0.3–1.3 cm)**

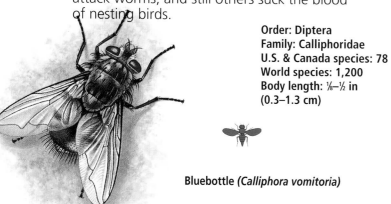

Bluebottle (*Calliphora vomitoria*)

Syrphid Flies

On any sunny day during the summer you will be able to see syrphid flies. Spend a while watching their amazing aerial acrobatics. A syrphid fly can move suddenly in any direction, including backward, or hover over a flower head. Look for these flies on flat-topped flower clusters as they feed on pollen and nectar. Although they look like bees and wasps, they cannot hurt you because they do not sting. In North America the larvae of *Mesogramma polita* sometimes damage corn crops, but the larvae of most species are useful and eat thousands of insects, especially aphids.

**Order: Diptera
Family: Syrphidae
U.S. & Canada species: 874
World species: 6,000
Body length: 1/8–1 1/2 in
(0.15–3.8 cm)**

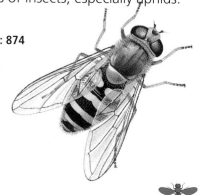

The hover fly (*Syrphus vitripennis*) can hover like a tiny helicopter.

Humpbacked Flies

These small humpbacked flies scuttle about on compost heaps, rotting fungi, and around the nests of rodents and ants. If you use your sweep net in such locations, you may find one of these flies scuttling among the assorted insects you have caught. As with all small insects, you need to observe these flies closely and patiently. The larvae of some humpbacked flies are internal parasites of other insects, spiders, snails, or millipedes. A few are pests of cultivated mushrooms.

Order: Diptera
Family: Phoridae
U.S. & Canada species: 360
World species:
3,000
Body length: ¹⁄₁₆–⅛ in
(0.15–0.3 cm)

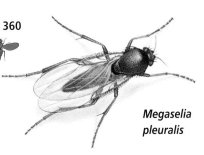

Megaselia pleuralis

Moth & Sand Flies

Both families are widely distributed through many habitats. The larval form of many species is unknown, and many other psychodid species remain undescribed. Some moth flies, which are sometimes called owl midges (subfamily: Psychodinae), are nocturnal and are attracted to lights. You may find some on your windows in spring and summer. Adult moth flies do not bite.

Sand flies (subfamily: Phlebotominae) feed on the blood of humans and many other vertebrates. They also carry germs that cause diseases in many tropical and subtropical regions of the world.

Order: Diptera
Family: Psychodidae
U.S. & Canada species: 90
World species: 1,000
Body length: ¹⁄₂₅–⅛ in
(1 mm–0.3 cm)

Moth fly *(Psychoda alternata)*

Leafminer Flies

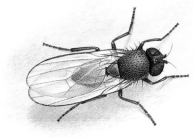

You are more likely to find the signs of their larvae than to see the adults, simply because these flies have no easy recognition features. The adults lay their eggs in plant tissue and their larvae make tunnels, or mines, between the upper and lower leaf surfaces. Species of *Liriomyza* are very destructive to tomatoes, cucumbers, squashes, celery, and other important plant species in North America. If you search through the leaves of holly between September and May, you should be able to find the work of the holly leafminer. Try keeping some mined leaves from a variety of plants in a sealed container (see page 65). In a while the adult flies, and even some of their parasites, may appear.

Leafminer
(Agromyza reptans)

Order: Diptera—Family: Agromyzidae
U.S. & Canada species: 188—World species: 2,000
Body length: ¹⁄₁₆–¼ in (0.15–0.6 cm)

Muscid Flies

You have certainly seen one of these flies land on the window or your food, or noticed them walking upside down on the ceiling. As they feed on decaying material and excrement, many of them spread germs that cause such diseases as cholera, typhoid fever, and dysentery. The female lays eggs in masses on rotting plant or animal matter. They hatch into larvae, which are commonly known as maggots. While we may not like the habits of the housefly (*Musca domestica*, shown here), we can admire how perfectly they are adapted to their way of life.

Order: Diptera
Family: Muscidae
U.S. & Canada
species: 697
World species: 4,000
Body length: ¹⁄₁₆–½ in
(0.15–1.3 cm)

Found Almost Everywhere

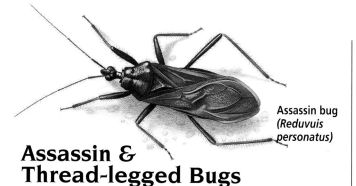

Assassin bug
(Reduvuis personatus)

Assassin & Thread-legged Bugs

All types of vegetation provide habitat for this family. Assassin bugs are well named because they hunt and kill all kinds of insects by sucking out their juice. A few species suck the blood of birds and mammals. Some species lie in wait to ambush prey, while others actively hunt for their food. Many species mimic the appearance and color pattern of their prey. A few assassin bug species collect plant resins on their front legs to attract and snare prey.
Order: Hemiptera—Family: Reduviidae
U.S. & Canada species: 110—World species: 5,500
Body length: ¼–1½ in (0.6–3.8 cm)

Leafhoppers

This is a large family. Some scientists believe that almost every plant species has at least one species of leafhopper eating it. All of them suck plant juices. The redbanded leafhopper (*Graphocephala coccinea*, shown here) is found on blackberry and other ornamental plants in North America. Females lay up to 300 eggs in the tissues of the host plant. The nymphs produce large amounts of honeydew which certain species, known as sharpshooters, can expel rapidly on to leaves. Many species produce up to five distinct types of sound. In this way they recognize their own species and find a mate. Many species are serious pests of crops and other important plants.
Order: Hemiptera—Family: Cicadellidae
U.S. & Canada species: 2,700
World species: 21,000
Body length: ½₀–½ in (1.3 mm–1.3 cm)

Aphids or Plant Lice

You can almost always see these tiny insects on plants. They are all suckers of plant sap. Aphids are pests on just about every crop and cultivated plant species. They also damage plants by passing on virus diseases. Because they suck in so much sweet plant sap, they produce a lot of sugary waste. This "honeydew" is often collected by ants (see page 11).
Order: Hemiptera
Family: Aphididae
U.S. & Canada species: 1,351
World species: 2,250
Body length: ⅟₁₆–¼ in (0.15–0.6 cm)

Garden black fly
(Aphis fabae)

Treehoppers

Many treehoppers have strange humps, spines, and other projections from the back of the thorax. If you touch one gently, you will see it hop. Some species look very much like thorns, as does the buffalo treehopper (*Stictocephala bisonia*, shown here), and this disguise helps them to pass unnoticed as part of a plant. This species was introduced to Europe in the early 1900's, and is often found on apple, willow, hawthorn, and lime trees. The nymphs of all species excrete honeydew, and many are attended by ants (see page 11) who gather the sweet liquid. In return, the ants guard the treehopper nymphs from attack. There is evidence of maternal care; the females of many species guard the young nymphs from attack.
Order: Hemiptera
Family: Membracidae
U.S. & Canada species: 258
World species: 2,500
Body length: ⅜ in (1 cm)

Psyllids

Each species belonging to this family lives on one plant or on a few, closely related plants. Some lay stalked eggs on plant surfaces, while others lay eggs inside plants. All members of this family are serious pests because they suck plant juices. They can also transmit virus diseases to such plants as tomatoes, potatoes, apples, and pears. The pear sucker (*Psylla pyricola*, shown here) is a pest on pear crops. Some members of this family also cause galls to form on leaves. These insects use their hind legs to jump.

Order: Hemiptera—Family: Psyllidae
U.S. & Canada species: 260—World species: 1,500
Body length: ¹⁄₁₆–¼ in (0.15–0.6 cm)

Minute Pirate Bugs

This is a family that lives in a variety of habitats, such as in flowers, under bark, in vegetation, leaf litter, and fungi. Others live in mammals' burrows, bird nests, bat caves, and grain stores. Many prey on small insects, while others are herbivorous (they eat plants). Despite their very small size they can give a very nasty bite if handled. Some species are useful because they eat red spider mites, aphids, and scale insects (see page 75).

Order: Hemiptera
Family: Anthocoridae
U.S. & Canada species: 85
World species: 500
Body length: ¹⁄₁₆–¼ in (0.15–0.6 cm)

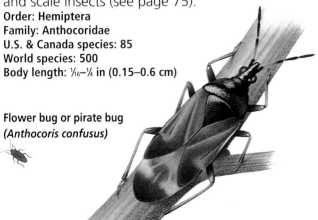

Flower bug or pirate bug
(*Anthocoris confusus*)

Plant Bugs

This family is found in every habitat from ground level to tree tops and on every type of vegetation. This family is the largest of the true bugs. The habits of various species vary enormously. You can come across some by simply looking carefully on plants, or perhaps find some in your beating tray (see page 52). A few species give off scents, which are like the alarm scents given off by ants. These serve as a protective device. Some species can feed on prey caught in spider webs.

Order: Hemiptera—Family: Miridae
U.S. & Canada species: 1,950
World species: 7,000
Body length: ¹⁄₁₆–½ in
(0.15–1.3 cm)

European tarnished plant bug
(*Lygus rugulipennis*)

Stink Bugs

The common name for these insects comes from their ability to produce very strong-smelling fluids when disturbed. These fluids repel enemies, can stain skin, and even produce bad headaches in sensitive people. Stink bugs live on herbaceous plants, shrubs, and trees in a wide range of habitats. Most are herbivores (plant-eaters), but some are carnivorous. In many species the female will guard her eggs and shepherd the young nymphs together, covering them with her body when danger threatens.

Order: Hemiptera
Family: Pentatomidae
U.S. & Canada
species: 250
World species: 5,250
Body length: ¼–1½ in
(0.6–3.8 cm)

Green stink bug
(*Zicrona caerula*)

Common, Paper, & Potter Wasps

These are easy to recognize as "real" wasps with their black and yellow, white, or red markings. Social wasps—those that live in groups—are some of nature's most elegant architects. Their nests, where a queen, males, and sterile female workers form a colony, are made by the workers chewing up wood fibers or paper. They feed their larvae on chewed insects, which they capture alive. The adults feed on nectar and other sugar-rich foods.

Potter wasps do not live in colonies. They collect mud or clay and make vase-shaped nests under ground, or in plant stems. They then paralyze a caterpillar and suspend it from the roof as preserved food for the larvae. Watch them, but be careful not to touch: they sting.

Order: Hymenoptera
Family: Vespidae
U.S. & Canada species: 415
World species: 17,000
Body length: ¼–1 in (0.6–2.5 cm)

German yellow jacket
(*Vespula germanica*)

Leafcutting & Mason Bees

Members of this large family of bees are common everywhere in areas where there is plenty of dead wood or pithy plant stems to provide nest sites. Most species are solitary. They collect mud, resin, leaf matter, or plant hairs to line their larval cells. If you search carefully on rosebushes in parks or yards during June and July, you may find almost circular holes cut into the leaves. This is the work of a leafcutting bee.

The alfalfa leafcutting bee (*Megachile rotundata*, shown above) was accidentally introduced from Eastern Europe to North America. It is now managed commercially for alfalfa pollination.

Some types of mason bees make their nests in rotting wood or snail shells. Other types build up cells of mud on walls or stones.

Order: Hymenoptera—Family: Megachilidae
U.S. & Canada species: 682—World species: 3,000
Body length: ¼–¾ in (0.6–2 cm)

Plasterer & Yellow-faced Bees

If you use your magnifying glass, you may see the structures called hairs which cover the bodies of these and all other families of bees.

Plasterer bees make simple nest burrows in the ground, or in natural cavities in stones and bricks.

Yellow-faced bees nest in the pith of plant stems, the empty burrows of wood-boring insects, and plant galls. Unlike plasterer bees, they do not have pollen baskets on their legs; instead they swallow the pollen with nectar to carry it to their nest. They then bring it up to fill the larval cells with food.

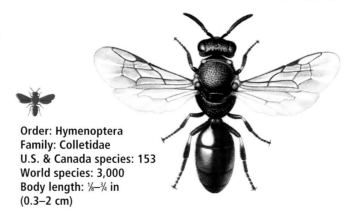

Order: Hymenoptera
Family: Colletidae
U.S. & Canada species: 153
World species: 3,000
Body length: ⅛–¾ in (0.3–2 cm)

Hylaeus bisinuatus is a yellow-faced bee, although it doesn't have a yellow face.

Mining or Andrenid Bees

Look for these bees in any flower-filled habitat in spring and early summer. As early as March you will see them on dandelions, daisies, and willow catkins. You may find tiny mounds of soil—signs of their burrow-building—on your lawn or in grassy, sunny banks. Although they are solitary bees, some species tend to make their burrows in large groups. They put pellets of mixed pollen and nectar in their burrows as food for the larvae. Some species are parasitized by cuckoo bees (see page 50). Mining and andrenid bees are common pollinators of spring flowers.

Order: Hymenoptera
Family: Andrenidae
U.S. & Canada
species: 1,200
World species: 4,000
Body length: ⅛–¾ in
(0.3–2 cm)

Andrena clarkella

Halictid or Sweat Bees

Only some species are attracted to sweat in addition to the normal diet of pollen and nectar. The bees in this family will sting, but the sting is not very painful. Some species are solitary; others are semi-social. The female is long-lived and often guards her pollen-stored cells until the young bees emerge. Most make burrows in firm soil, such as garden paths, especially with clay or sandy soils. The species of sweat bee (*Halictus rubicundus*) shown here is a typical member of this family.

Order: Hymenoptera
Family: Halictidae
U.S. & Canada
species: 502
World species: 5,000
Body length: ⅛–½ in
(0.3–1.3 cm)

Bumble Bees & Honey Bees

Bumble bees are those large, furry, buzzing bees that visit flowers throughout the summer. In sunny weather in March and April, watch for a large queen bumble that has just come out of winter hibernation. She will make a mossy nest on or under the ground. Her 300 or 400 eggs will first produce sterile worker bees to build up the colony and collect food.

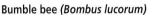

Bumble bee *(Bombus lucorum)*

Honey bees are much smaller and often start a colony in a hollow tree or roof space. They are also kept in hives by beekeepers. A single queen may lay tens of thousands of eggs to produce workers, and up to 2,000 eggs to produce males or drones. Honey bees collect nectar and pollen from flowers. They store pollen and the honey they make from nectar in thousands of wax cells which make a comb.

Order: Hymenoptera—Family: Apidae
U.S. & Canada species: 57—World species: 1,000
Body length: ⅛–1 in (0.3–2.5 cm)

Common Sawflies

Sawflies are not flies at all. They are in the same insect order as wasps, ants, and bees. Unlike those creatures, a sawfly has no waist. The name of these insects refers to the sawlike ovipositor (egg-laying organ) of the females. With it they cut slits in leaves, twigs, or shoots of their host plants and lay their eggs there.

Order: Hymenoptera
Family: Tenthredinidae
U.S. & Canada species: 731
World species: 4,000
Body length: ⅛–¾ in
(0.3–3 cm)

 Strongylogaster macula

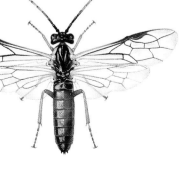

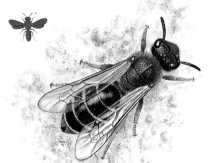

Blue, Copper, and Hairstreak Butterflies

We do not know a lot about the life cycles of many of these brilliantly colored, iridescent blue, copper, or purplish butterflies. About one-third live in association with ants in a variety of habitats. The butterfly larvae produce a sugary fluid that the ants eat. In return the ants guard them. The caterpillars of some species even feed on the larvae in the ants' nest. As many of this family are very beautiful, they have been over-collected and are close to extinction. Many are now protected by law.

Order: Lepidoptera
Family: Lycaenidae
U.S. & Canada species: 150
World species: 4,000
Wingspan: ½–2 in (1.3–5 cm)

American copper
(Lycaena phlaeas)

Tiger & Ermine Moths

Tiger moths are mainly nocturnal, heavy-bodied, hairy, and often brightly colored. The bright colors are a warning to their predators that they are distasteful; some are even poisonous. The best time to search for the garden tiger moth (*Arctia caja*, shown here) is when it is on the wing in July and August. The cinnabar moth (*Tyria jacobaea*) has been introduced from Europe to North American Pacific states to control St.-John's-wort.

Ermine moths tend to be pale or white with small black spots or patches. Because of the variety of their food plants, they are found in a wide variety of habitats. The caterpillars are covered with hairs that cause a rash in humans.

Order: Lepidoptera
Family: Arctiidae
U.S. & Canada species: 264
World species: 2,500
Wingspan: ¾–2¾ in (2–7 cm)

Agonopterix heracliana

Oecophorid Moths

Most of these moths can be found in a variety of habitats in association with their host plants. A very few species are found indoors where they may be pests of wool and other textiles. Not much is known about the caterpillars of some species, but some eat plants or are fungus feeders, and others may feed on decaying matter.
Order: Lepidoptera
Family: Oecophoridae
U.S. & Canada species: 230
World species: 3,500
Wingspan: ¼–1⅛ in (0.6–2.8 cm)

Brush-footed Butterflies

This is a family of beautiful and colorful butterflies. You see them flying and visiting flowers to drink the nectar on sunny days. They are found everywhere—especially in flower-rich meadows, woodland clearings, and yards—except very dry deserts and polar regions. Their caterpillars are generally spiny and feed on nettles, thistles, sunflowers, and other plants. Look among stinging nettles in July and August and you should find larvae of the red admiral and mourning cloak butterflies. Members of this family, like the painted lady (*Vanessa cardui*, shown here), undertake migrations, and some species, like the small tortoiseshell, hibernate.
Order: Lepidoptera
Family: Nymphalidae
U.S. & Canada species: 150
World species: 3,500
Wingspan: 1⅛–4¼ in (2.8–10.8 cm)

Tortricid Moths

Species of this large family of smallish moths show a multitude of cryptic patterns on their wings. Some of the patterns make these moths look like bark, lichen, bird droppings, or bits of leaves. They are found in a wide variety of habitats. There are many pest species in the family, notably the codling moth (*Cydia pomonella*, shown here), introduced to North America over 200 years ago. The caterpillars of some species bore into stems and leaves, and a few cause galls.

Order: Lepidoptera
Family: Tortricidae
U.S. & Canada species: 1,053
World species: 4,500
Wingspan: ¼–1¼ in
(0.6–3.2 cm)

Pyralid Moths

The front wings of this family are usually oblong or triangular with closely packed scales. In some species the front of the head looks as if it has a small snout. This is the third largest family of moths, so there is a huge range of color, shape, and size in the different species. Many are pests: the caterpillar of the European corn borer (*Ostrinia nubilalis*, adult shown here) damages young corn. This species was accidentally introduced to North America in the early 1900's. Others attack corn, sunflowers, apples, cabbage, and other food crops.

Order: Lepidoptera
Family: Pyralidae
U.S. & Canada species: 1,374
World species: 17,500
Wingspan: ½–1½ in
(1.3–3.8 cm)

White, Sulfur, & Orange-tip Butterflies

This family contains some of the world's most common butterflies. Their habitats range from woodlands to meadows and from mountains to sea level. Caterpillars of the best-known species feed on cabbages and similar plants. In good summer weather small whites breed so fast that they become pests on cabbage crops. This species is one of the most crop-damaging butterflies. Other species feed on alders, hawthorns, and willows. Look for orange-tips flying along hedges in early summer. Search for the sulfurs along hedges that include the spiny shrub called buckthorn.

Order: Lepidoptera—Family: Pieridae
U.S. & Canada species: 60
World species: 1,000
Wingspan: ¾–2¾ in
(2–7 cm)

Small white
(*Pieris rapae*)

Noctuid Moths

Species from this enormous family of moths can be found all over the world. With a medium-sized wingspan, mostly 1¾–2½ inches (4.5–5 centimeters), they are dull in color with narrowish front wings. The antennae are hairlike in females, but brushlike in males. Males often have a tuft of hairs at the end of the abdomen. They fly at night and can be found in almost every kind of habitat. Some species have special hearing organs which help the moths to detect and avoid bats. The dark sword-grass moth (*Agrotis ipsilon*, shown here) is widespread in North America.

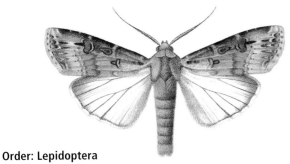

Order: Lepidoptera
Family: Noctuidae
U.S. & Canada species: 3,000
World species: 20,000
Wingspan: ½–3⅛ in (1.3–8 cm)

Measuringworm Moths

Peppered moth (*Biston betularia*)

The caterpillars of this enormous family move by a looping motion. A measuring worm caterpillar draws its hind end up to meet the front end in a loop, then pushes the front end forward. This gives the family its name, *Geometridae*, meaning "earth-measuring." The adult moths can be found almost everywhere that plants grow, and in summer many will fly in and settle on lighted windows. Very many species are pests of trees and crops. The winter moth (*Operophtera brumata*, shown here) is a typical pest species, introduced to North America from Europe. It particularly damages apple trees.
Order: Lepidoptera—Family: Geometridae
U.S. & Canada species: 1,400
World species: 12,000—Wingspan: ½–1¾ in (1.3–4.5 cm)

Hawk or Sphinx Moths

The moths in this family rest with swept-back wings, like the wings of a fighter plane. Many species visit garden and park flowers, such as petunias, at dusk. Hawk moths' habitats cover a great variety of wooded and open areas, including yards and parks, where their food—plants, trees, and flowers—may grow. Some species are serious crop pests. The tomato hornworm (*Manduca quinquemaculata*) of North America and the tobacco hornworm (*Manduca sexta*) are examples. Most species in this family are nocturnal feeders.

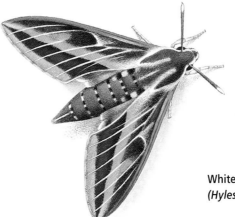

Order: Lepidoptera
Family: Sphingidae
U.S. & Canada species: 124
World species: 1,000
Wingspan: 1½–6 in (3.8–15.2 cm)

White-lined sphinx moth (*Hyles lineata*)

An Insect Safari

There are insects everywhere on Earth, from the cold tundra to the jungles and deserts of the tropics. So, regardless of where you are, a lot of insects are likely to be around. Remember, it is always best to observe rather than to touch or handle insects.

Insect watching

A good time to study insects such as bees, wasps, dragonflies, and butterflies is on a warm, sunny day when there is no wind. If you want to watch nighttime (nocturnal) insects such as moths, a warm, still summer evening is best.

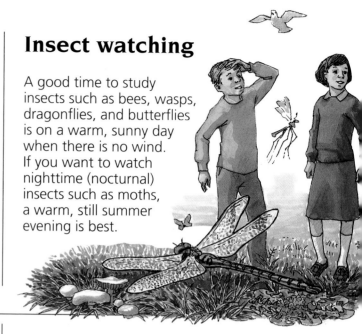

What to take

When you go looking for insects, it is a good idea to take these pieces of equipment with you:

1 **Magnifying lens:** helps you to look at small insects close up and in great detail. Buy a folding one that magnifies things 4 or 6 times (labeled x4 or x6). Wear it on a cord around your neck.
2 **Glass or plastic jars with holes bored in the lid:** useful if you find a large insect and want to put it somewhere safe while you look at it.
3 **Aspirator:** see opposite for how to make one.
4 **Aerial net:** for trapping butterflies and moths temporarily.
5 **Beating tray:** for investigating trees and bushes (see pages 52–53).
6 **Field notebook with pencils and pens:** make notes of the date, the time, the weather, where you go, and what you find.
7 **Lightweight backpack:** this is the most comfortable way to carry your equipment, and leaves your hands free.

Making an aspirator

An aspirator helps you to pick up and look at bugs and other small insects without harming them. It is quite easy to make an aspirator of your own.

1 **Take a piece of clear plastic** 4 inches (10 centimeters) square and roll it into a tube. Secure it with adhesive tape.

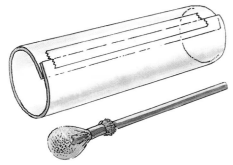

2 **You will also need two wide drinking straws** and a piece of gauze 2½ inches (about 6 centimeters) square. Place the gauze over the end of one of the straws and tape it in position.

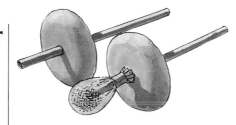

3 **With modeling clay or plasticine,** make two round blobs, each about the size of a ping-pong ball. Squash them flat into disks, then push one straw through the middle of each.

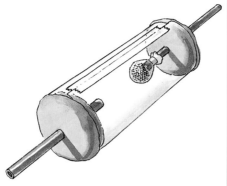

4 **Put one clay disk at each end of the plastic tube,** so that the gauze is inside the tube.

5 **When you suck at the straw with gauze on the other end,** air will rush into the plastic aspirator through the other straw. If you then gently hold your aspirator close to a bug and suck on the straw, the insect will be caught safely and quickly.

6 **Once you have finished looking,** release the insect by removing one end of the aspirator. Always try to put insects back where you found them.

7 **Remember to use your aspirator carefully,** and never try to catch spiders or large insects like butterflies, because you could harm them. **Do not try to catch insects that you know may sting or bite.**

Where to look

You probably don't need to look far on your insect safari to see a beetle on the ground or a bee at a flower. You can find other kinds of insects on leaves, plant stems, under stones, and under loose tree bark. Spend some time watching the insects that you find to see where they go and what they do. If you look carefully, you will learn lots more about the way they live.

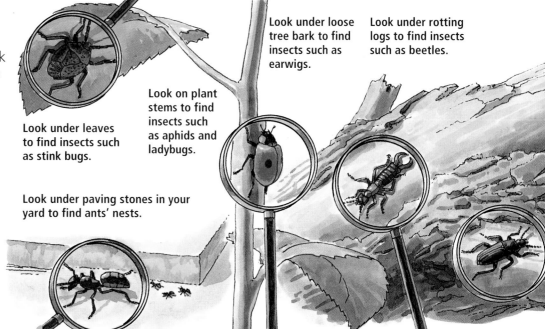

Look under leaves to find insects such as stink bugs.

Look on plant stems to find insects such as aphids and ladybugs.

Look under paving stones in your yard to find ants' nests.

Look under loose tree bark to find insects such as earwigs.

Look under rotting logs to find insects such as beetles.

Grasslands

Wide, open grasslands once made up most of what are now the Midwestern United States and the prairie provinces of Canada. Most of this land is now planted with crops, and only remnants of the original grasslands remain.

But you will also find grasslands or prairies in the Southwest, California, and between the Rockies, the Sierra Nevada, and the Cascade range. Tall grasses are typical of eastern prairies; short grasses grow on western prairies. Tall grass is spectacular, particularly in spring when the wild flowers are blooming. This habitat includes hedges and all grassy areas rich in wild flowers.

This picture shows nine kinds of insects from this section. How many can you identify?

Soldier beetle, tumbling flower beetle, American monarch butterfly, seed bug, black scavenger fly, field grasshopper, planthopper, European mantid, wheat stem sawfly

Soldier Beetles

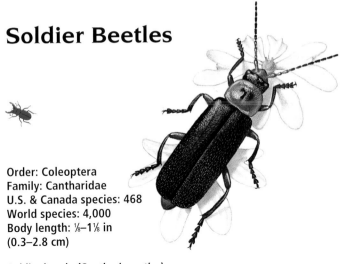

Order: Coleoptera
Family: Cantharidae
U.S. & Canada species: 468
World species: 4,000
Body length: ⅛–1⅛ in
(0.3–2.8 cm)

Soldier beetle *(Cantharis rustica)*

Some species of this family are very common, so you should easily find them. In warm sunshine, look for them on flowers, along roadsides, and at the edge of woodlands. The common family name comes from the resemblance of their coloring to old military uniforms. Although the adults of some species eat pollen and nectar, adults and their larvae hunt for prey on the ground. The soldier beetle in the picture can be found on grass and nettles, especially if you search for it in early summer. Birds rarely attack them—this is probably because of the beetle's bright yellow, red, or orange warning colors and nasty taste.

Tumbling Flower Beetles

Order: Coleoptera
Family: Mordellidae
U.S. & Canada species: 207
World species: 1,250
Body length: ¹⁄₁₆–⅔ in
(0.15–1.6 cm)

Look for these beetles on plants of the daisy family and on flowers with flat tops like cow-parsnip and wild carrot. In warm sunshine, these beetles may be found at rest on tree trunks. The reason for their common name is their habit of tumbling off their resting place when disturbed. Adults feed on flowers, but some of their larvae burrow in plant stems or live in decaying wood, while others bore inside fungi. Members of this family are not pests.

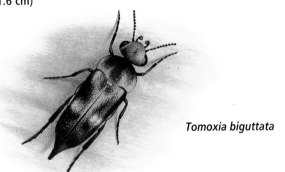

Tomoxia biguttata

Earth-boring Dung Beetles

As their name suggests, these beetles are found beneath dung of all kinds, on carrion, and in decaying wood or fungi. The adults dig out burrows many inches (or centimeters) deep and stock these tunnels with balls of dung. A single egg is laid on each ball. The larva feeds on the dung. Some species feed on plant material, but most of the family are valuable as scavengers and dung removers. Look for them around sunset on a warm evening.

Order: Coleoptera
Family: Geotrupidae
U.S. & Canada species: 51
World species: 550
Body length: ¼–1⅔ in
(0.6–4 cm)

The common dor beetle *(Geotrupes stercorarius)* flies in the evening and is attracted to light. The word "dor" comes from the ancient word meaning "drone," and refers to the humming flight of the beetle.

Fruit Flies

Search for these flies around flowers and vegetation. You may be fortunate enough to watch their courtship behavior. The males of many species walk to and fro in front of the females. As they do so, they slowly wave one of their attractively patterned wings while holding the other upright. Many of their larvae live inside soft fruits, in the flower heads of daisies and related plants, or as stem-miners, leaf miners (see page 15), and gall-formers. As pest species, some attack citrus fruits, peaches, cherries, apples, walnuts, and melons. The Mediterranean fruit fly (*Ceratitis capitata*, shown here) is a very serious pest in subtropical and tropical regions.

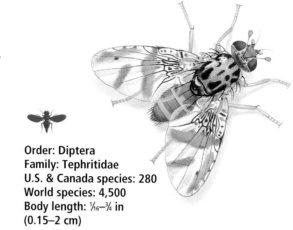

Order: Diptera
Family: Tephritidae
U.S. & Canada species: 280
World species: 4,500
Body length: 1/16–3/4 in
(0.15–2 cm)

Some species of fruit flies cause galls to form on thistles. You may find some if you search carefully. Each gall contains several growing larvae.

March Flies

Order: Diptera
Family: Bibionidae
U.S. & Canada species: 78
World species: 780
Body length: 1/4–1/2 in (0.6–1.3 cm)

These insects were originally called St. Mark's flies because they are seen in swarms around April 25, which is the feast day of St. Mark. The females lay 200 to 300 eggs belowground, and their larvae eat all kinds of organic material and plant roots. Their habitats are yards, flower-rich pastures, and similar places. The St. Mark's fly (*Bibio marci*, shown here) is a typical member of the family. You may see one or more of these hairy-bodied flies flying slowly with its legs dangling down on a sunny April day.

Frit Flies

Their habitat is grassy meadows and among overgrown plants, flowers, and decaying organic matter. The adults of this family eat nectar, prey on root aphids, or eat the eggs of spiders, moths, and other insects. A few, however, are serious pests of farm crops. The larvae of most species are herbivorous. Those of the *Oscinella frit*, shown here, damage grain crops by boring into them.

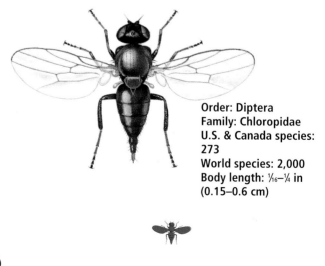

Order: Diptera
Family: Chloropidae
U.S. & Canada species: 273
World species: 2,000
Body length: 1/16–1/4 in (0.15–0.6 cm)

Soldier Flies

This is a family of robust, metallic-sheened flies favoring a damp habitat. Look for them sitting on flowers of willow and hawthorn and flowers with flat tops, like water hemlock. You may hear some flying with a wasplike hum over marshy ground from June to August. The name soldier fly comes from their armor of spines on various body parts. Some of their larvae, living under bark, may control bark beetles (see page 38).

Order: Diptera
Family: Stratiomyidae
U.S. & Canada species: 260
World species: 1,800
Body length: ¹⁄₁₆–⅔ in (0.15–1.6 cm)

Sargus cuprarius

Anthomyiid Flies

This is a very large family of rather ordinary-looking flies, which somewhat resemble houseflies (see page 15). Their adult food varies, ranging from pollen and nectar to small insects. Some of their larvae may be found

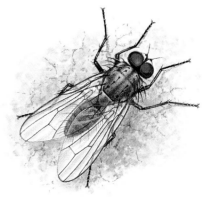

The larvae of the bean seed fly *(Delia platura)*, called seed corn maggots, damage many plants.

as stem-borers, gall-formers, and leafminers (see page 15), while others live in rotting seaweed or bird droppings. The maggots of a few species of *Delia* damage onions, turnips, cabbage, grain, and carnations, and have become serious pests. Since they are so common, it should not be too long before you see one.

Order: Diptera—Family: Anthomyiidae
U.S. & Canada species: 600—World species: 1,500
Body length: ¹⁄₁₆–½ in (0.15–1.3 cm)

Black Scavenger Flies

Members of this family are to be seen on flowers, vegetation, and around dung or decaying plant and animal matter. Adult males display their wing tips by walking to and fro and flicking their wings outward. This is done to attract females. Whenever you are watching an insect, look out for interesting behavior. Make notes in your field notebook when you observe something (see page 24).

Order: Diptera
Family: Sepsidae
U.S. & Canada species: 34
World species: 250
Body length: ¹⁄₁₆–¼ in (0.15–0.6 cm)

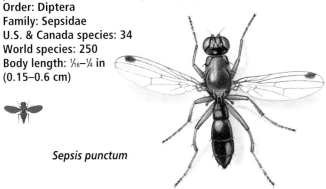

Sepsis punctum

Dung Flies

You are most likely to encounter these flies around areas where cattle are kept. Avoid these flies because they carry disease germs. Their common name comes from the habit of most members of this family of laying their eggs in animal droppings. Adult dung flies all kill and eat small insects. While the habitats of many flies may seem unpleasant to us, their way of life helps to recycle materials back into the ecosystem.

Order: Diptera
Family: Scathophagidae
U.S. & Canada species: 148
World species: 250
Body length: 1⅛–½ in (0.3–1.3 cm)

Yellow dung fly
(Scathophaga stercoraria)

Spittle Bug

In the summer, you have probably seen a small, white, frothy mass on grass stems and leaves. It is often called "cuckoo spit." If you take a grass stem and gently stroke away the bubbles, you will discover the nymph of a spittle bug. The foam, which is a form of protection, is a glandular secretion mixed with the bug's waste (honeydew). Some birds have learned to pull the nymphs out and eat them. Adult spittle bugs, like froghoppers (see opposite page), are active jumpers. In North America two species attack pines.

Order: Hemiptera
Family: Cercopidae
U.S. & Canada species: 23
World species: 850
Body length: ¼–¾ in (0.6–2 cm)

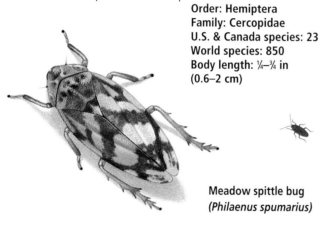

Meadow spittle bug
(*Philaenus spumarius*)

Delphacid Planthoppers

This family is common everywhere in grasslands, meadows, pastures, and woodland margins. Adults and nymphs feed on plant sap. Although grasses and sedges (wetland grasses) are their main host plants, they also attack other plants. Some species have become serious crop pests; the sugar-cane leafhopper, for example, was accidentally introduced from Australia to Hawaii, where it caused terrible damage to sugar cane. It was brought under control by using a small plant bug that sucked the eggs of the leafhopper. The corn hopper (*Peregrinus maidis*) spreads virus disease in corn throughout North America.

Order: Hemiptera
Family: Delphacidae
U.S. & Canada species: 145
World species: 1,800
Body length: ¹⁄₁₆–⅓ in (0.15–0.8 cm)

Planthopper
(*Javesella pellucida*)

Scentless Plant Bugs

You may find members of this family on weeds and overgrown vegetation in old fields and other similar undisturbed habitats. These bugs lack scent glands, which is how the family gets its common name. A few live in trees, so look out for them when you use your beating tray (see page 52). Like so many other bugs, they suck the juices of leaves, seeds, and fruit of their host plants. The best time to look for them is late summer and early fall. The hyaline grass bug (*Liorhyssus hyalinus*, shown here) varies in color from black to yellow. Its main food is daisies.

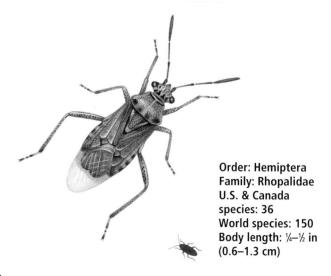

Order: Hemiptera
Family: Rhopalidae
U.S. & Canada species: 36
World species: 150
Body length: ¼–½ in (0.6–1.3 cm)

Damsel Bugs

These bugs are found in a wide range of habitats, from the ground to vegetation of all kinds, wherever small insects are available as prey. They catch and suck fluids from aphids, caterpillars, and many other kinds of soft-bodied insects. You may find some by sweep-netting dry grasslands, such as hay fields. Do not handle them, because some members of this family can bite. They are useful to humans because they help to control natural insect populations, which include pest species.

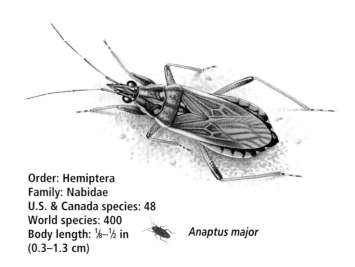

Order: Hemiptera
Family: Nabidae
U.S. & Canada species: 48
World species: 400
Body length: ⅛–½ in
(0.3–1.3 cm)

Anaptus major

Froghoppers

Adult froghoppers are active jumpers, like the spittle bugs (see opposite page). Many species are pests and can damage plants by their feeding activities. Their habitat is meadows, scrub, and woodlands, all with plenty of vegetation. Their nymphs suck sap from plant stems. This activity produces a frothy foam that helps protect the nymphs from predators. This protects them from some predators and also prevents evaporation. The *Cercopis vulnerata*, shown here, illustrates this species' warning colors, which tell any enemy it is dangerous to eat because it is poisonous.

Order: Hemiptera
Family: Cercopidae
U.S. & Canada species: 33
World species: 1,400
Body length: ¼–¾ in (0.6–2 cm)

Seed Bugs

Seed bugs are usually found in leaf litter, under stones, or in low-growing vegetation, such as stinging nettles. Most of the family are seed-eaters, who use their strong, spined front legs to grasp their food. Some are plant-sap suckers and a few are hunters of other insects. They produce sounds which may help to attract a mate. They use well-developed scent glands to protect themselves against enemies. Many species are pests to garden plants and farm crops and cause great damage. The chinch bug (*Blissus leucopterus*), shown here, can damage corn, wheat, rye, oats, barley, and other grain crops in North America.

Order: Hemiptera
Family: Lygaeidae
U.S. & Canada species: 300
World species: 3,500
Body length: ⅛–¾ in
(0.3–2 cm)

Grasslands

Mantids

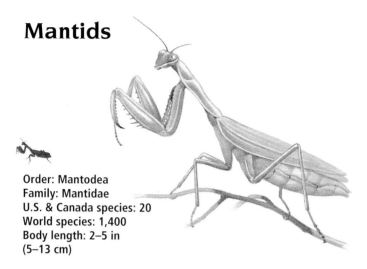

Order: Mantodea
Family: Mantidae
U.S. & Canada species: 20
World species: 1,400
Body length: 2–5 in
(5–13 cm)

These insects hold their front legs in an attitude of prayer, which is how they got their name "praying mantis." But they are simply waiting to seize any passing insects with their spiked legs. They are probably the only insects that can look over their shoulders. Their habitat is almost anywhere that has a regular supply of insect prey. They are able to snatch flying insects out of the air. The European mantid (*Mantis religiosa*, shown here) was introduced to North America about 1899. It is now common in many parts of the country. If handled, it tries to bite, but is not dangerous. A female lays a couple of hundred eggs, contained in an egg case called an "ootheca," which she attaches to a plant.

Short-horned Grasshoppers & Locusts

Their common name describes their short antennae. They are found on the ground and on plants in meadows, hedges, and many other similar places in summertime, and are plant-eaters. If you walk slowly through a field on a sunny summer day, you will hear them "singing." They sing by rubbing their ridged hind legs against the hard edge of their front wings. The desert locust, one of the most damaging pests in the world, belongs to this family. A very large group of short-horned grasshoppers in North America is *Melanoplus*. There are around 300 species in this genus.

Order: Orthoptera
Family: Acrididae
U.S. & Canada species: 550
World species: 9,000
Body length: ⅓–3⅛ in
(0.8–7.8 cm)

Field grasshopper
(*Chorthippus brunneus*)

Stem Sawflies

Like all sawflies, the female stem sawfly has an ovipositor (egg-laying tube), which is modified to function like a saw. She literally saws into plant stems to make a slit in which to lay her eggs. The larvae look very much like the caterpillars of moths or butterflies. The larvae burrow inside the stems of grasses, willows, and other plants. Unlike other sawfly larvae, their legs are very small. Look for the slow-flying adults around yellow flowers. The wheat stem sawfly (*Cephus pygmaeus*, shown here) is a pest of grain crops; it was introduced to North America from Europe. Although it looks a little like a wasp, a closer look shows it has no "waist."

Order: Hymenoptera—Family: Cephidae
U.S. & Canada species: 12—World species: 100
Body length: ⅛–¾ in (0.3–2 cm)

Skippers

This family name refers to their active, rapid and darting flight patterns—they almost "skip" from flower to flower. You will find them in habitats where their caterpillars' food—various types of plants—grows. Although these are mainly grasses, such species as the dingy skipper are found on birdsfoot trefoil and other plants. Unlike other butterfly caterpillars, this family lives within a shelter of silk-tied or rolled leaves. The caterpillars pupate at the plant's base within a silken web. You should search for skippers on a sunny day in meadows, rough grasslands, woods, and hay fields.

Order: Lepidoptera
Family: Hesperioidae
U.S. & Canada species: 300
World species: 3,500
Wingspan: ⅛–2½ in
(0.3–6.3 cm)

European skipper *(Thymelicus lineola)*

Milkweed Butterflies

The name "milkweed" refers to the plant eaten by this butterfly's caterpillars. The American monarch butterfly (*Danaus plexippus*, shown here) occasionally reaches European shores. It is an amazing migration for so delicate a creature, but they regularly travel from Canada to California, Florida, and Mexico, where vast numbers assemble and roost. Their bright colors are a warning that they taste nasty, so birds leave them alone.

Order: Lepidoptera—Family: Danaidae
U.S. & Canada species: 4—World species: 200
Wingspan: 2⅓–4 in (5.8–10 cm)

Swallowtails

This family includes the very large bird-wing butterflies of Southeast Asia, the largest butterflies in the world. Swallowtails are perhaps the loveliest of all butterflies. They are beautifully marked with yellow, orange, red, green, or blue. Their caterpillars feed on many plants, including angelica, fennel, and wild carrot.

Parnassian butterflies do not have hind-wing tails and are white or gray with red-and-black markings. They are found in high places in North America and Europe. Many of these families are protected by the law in parts of the world. However, it is even more important to protect their habitats, or they will become extinct.

Order: Lepidoptera
Family: Papilionidae
Species: 35
World species: 600
Wingspan: 2–5 in
(5–13 cm)

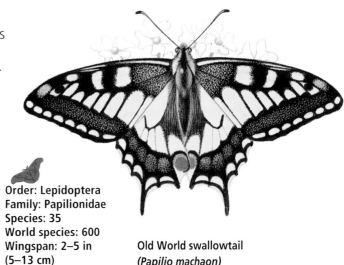

Old World swallowtail
(Papilio machaon)

Attracting Insects

A yard makes a very good nature reserve for insects. Even in the smallest yard you can find hundreds of different kinds of insects. A yard contains plenty of things for insects to feed on and a lot of places for insects to hide. See how many different insects you can find in your garden. If you enjoy watching them, it is easy to encourage even more to visit your yard or window box.

Insect favorites

Butterflies, bees, and other flying insects visit flowers to feed on their sweet nectar. Buddleia, thistles, and other purple flowers are especially popular. In fact, buddleia is such a favorite with butterflies, such as red admirals, that it is nicknamed the "butterfly bush."

A wild corner

Ask your parents if you can let a small area of the yard grow wild. You could also scatter some wild flower seeds in your wild patch. You can buy packets of wild flower seeds at your local garden center. Don't dig up plants from the wild.

The wild plants that you grow will encourage all sorts of interesting insects to move in. Nettles provide food for caterpillars, while dandelions, daisies, and buttercups attract bees and butterflies by offering them nectar to sip. In return, the insects help the flowers to reproduce.

Bees' homes

To attract solitary bees to your backyard, you could make some bee nesting burrows, using a can, large drinking straws, and a piece of wire.

1 **Find a clean, empty can and enough large drinking straws to fill the can.** If the straws are longer than the can, ask an adult to cut off the ends so that they are all about 1 inch (2.5 centimeters) shorter than the can. This will create a lip to help keep the rain out.

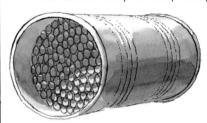

2 **Fill the can with enough straws** so that they cannot move around inside.

Moth feast

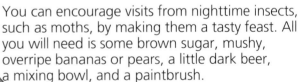

You can encourage visits from nighttime insects, such as moths, by making them a tasty feast. All you will need is some brown sugar, mushy, overripe bananas or pears, a little dark beer, a mixing bowl, and a paintbrush.

1 **Put 1 pound (about 1/2 kilogram) of brown sugar** into a mixing bowl and add one or two mushy bananas or pears. Add a little dark beer and stir the mixture well.

2 **At dusk, go into the yard** with your mixture and a paintbrush. Paint some strips about 2 inches (about 5 centimeters) wide and 18 inches (about 45 centimeters) long on to the bark of a few trees.

3 **Wait patiently** for your hungry visitors to arrive.

4 **Take a small flashlight** with you. It will help you to watch the insects when it gets dark.

3 **Take the piece of wire and wind it** around the middle of the can. Fasten it so that you have enough wire left to hang the can up.

4 **Now ask an adult to help you hang the bee home** under the roof of a shed or garage, or in a tree.
5 **Watch from a distance.** In a few days you should see some bees making their nests inside. Remember, bees can sting you!
6 **To make an even simpler bee home**, find a rotten log and ask an adult to drill a lot of holes in it for you. Place the log on a low wall, or attach it to the side of a shed, and wait for the bees to arrive.

Make a mini pond

If you don't have a yard, or if your yard is too small for a pond, why not make a mini pond? Simply fill a large, old, plastic bowl with water and add a few small water plants, then wait and see what happens.

Making a pond

One of the most interesting ways to attract dragonflies is to make a pond. This is quite simple to do, and it also makes a perfect habitat for water boatmen and water beetles. **Do not make a pond in an area where small children play. Do not make a pond if you live in an area prone to West Nile virus.**
1 **Decide where you want to put the pond.** Check with an adult before making a final decision.
2 **Ask an adult to help you dig a hollow** about 18 inches (45 centimeters) deep, using a garden spade.
3 **Buy a sheet of plastic pond lining** from your local garden center. It must be big enough to fill the hole and spread out over the edge of the pond by a few inches (or centimeters).

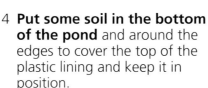

4 **Put some soil in the bottom of the pond** and around the edges to cover the top of the plastic lining and keep it in position.
5 **To plant your pond** you will need one or two pond plants in pots and some pond weed (like water milfoil). Ask your garden center for advice on what to plant.

6 **Secure the plant pots with stones, bricks, or other heavy objects** so that they don't move around, then fill the pond with water.
7 **It may take several months,** or even a year before insects begin to appear in your pond, but it's worth being patient. However, you may see midge and mosquito larvae within a few days in warm weather.

Woods & Forests

This habitat includes forests, woodlands, and forest clearings. Forests are large areas dominated by trees, which can be coniferous (cone-bearing evergreens), mostly in the West, or deciduous (trees that lose their leaves in fall, like oaks or walnuts), mostly in the East.

Woodlands are often small patches left over from a larger forest that may have once existed in the area. The environment inside a woods or forest is sheltered from winds and usually cool and damp. All kinds of wildlife can find shelter among the trees throughout the year. A lot of flowers may bloom in deciduous woods in spring, before the trees grow leaves. You will find bees and many other insects visiting these flowers for pollen and nectar.

Mature woods and forests with a lot of different trees and sunny clearings are the best places for you to find insects. You should look for them in every part of a tree: the leaves, roots, bark, wood, flowers, fruit, and so on. Did you know, for instance, that an average oak tree provides a living and home for more than 300 animal species? Most of these are insects.

As you explore a woods, look especially for strange growths on leaves, buds, and bark. These are formed by gall wasps. Search carefully through leaf litter as well, and you will find many other specialized insects. This picture shows 11 kinds of insects from this section. How many can you identify?

Spruce bark beetle, pleasing fungus beetle, European jewel beetle, common ringlet butterfly, glow worm, brown lacewing, greater horntail wasp, two-spotted lady beetle, gypsy moth, snakefly, eastern subterranean termite

Bark or Engraver Beetles

Spruce bark beetle
(Polygraphus poligraphus)

Members of this family are found on or near many coniferous and deciduous tree species. Bark beetles have been responsible for changing the appearance of the countryside. The larvae of some species spread Dutch elm disease by carrying a fungus infection which clogs the sap channels of the tree and kills it. You may find the signs of these beetles if you peel back the bark of fallen or dead trees (see page 47). Many species produce chemical attraction odors called "pheromones"; these attract many other beetles, and so cause a huge infection of the tree.

Order: Coleoptera—Family: Scolytidae
U.S. & Canada species: 500—World species: 9,000
Body length: 1/16–1/3 in (0.15–0.8 cm)

Metallic Wood-boring Beetles

This family includes many of the most beautiful beetles in the world. They look a little like click beetles (see page 76), but do not "jump." They are found in coniferous and deciduous woods. They are also called jewel beetles. Female jewel beetles lay eggs in wood, and the larvae chew tunnels in the roots and trunks of trees. Some species are leafminers, and some bore into plant stems. Biologists have evidence that these beetles possess infra-red detectors to locate burned areas where some lay their eggs. They react to disturbance by flying off, or by pretending to be dead.

European jewel beetle
(Melanophila acuminata)

Order: Coleoptera—Family: Buprestidae
U.S. & Canada species: 675—World species: 14,000
Body length: 1/16–2½ in (0.15–6.3 cm)

Deathwatch Beetles

These are small, brown or black beetles. Most measure about 1/8–1/4 inches (0.3–0.6 centimeters) long. Some species produce larvae which bore into wood, so they are known as woodworms. Their habitat is all kinds of wooden structure, either indoors or outside. The adult of some species attracts a mate by tapping its head against the walls of the tunnel inside the timber. Superstitious people believe the tapping foretells a death in a house, which gives this beetle its common name. Others attack stored tobacco, spices, and drugs. The furniture beetle (*Anobium punctatum*, shown here) is present in many old houses.

Order: Coleoptera
Family: Anobiidae
U.S. & Canada species: 299
World species: 1,500
Body length: 1/16–1/3 in (0.15–0.8 cm)

Horse & Deer Flies

Species of this family are also known as gadflies, clegs, and stouts. Their large, flattened heads and large eyes are distinctive. The adult blood-sucking females will be found around mammals. They approach their prey with great stealth and alight on hard-to-reach places. Using their bladelike mouthparts, they cut into the skin and feed on the blood. The males can be seen feeding on flower nectar. The eggs are laid on plants and trees near water. The bite of these flies can cause painful swellings and even allergic reactions in animals and people.

Order: Diptera
Family: Tabanidae
U.S. & Canada species: 350
World species: 4,100
Body length: 1/16–1⅛ in (0.15–2.8 cm)

Tabanus bovinus

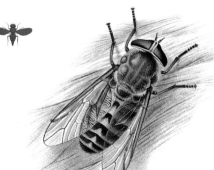

Tussock Moths

These typically dull-colored moths have no working mouthparts and they do not feed, living only days or weeks. Some tussock caterpillars have body hairs that can give you a severe skin rash. The caterpillars drop these irritating hairs all over their pupae to protect them. They are found in hedgerows, conifer and broad-leaf woodlands, and hop fields. The gypsy moth (*Lymantria dispar*, shown here) and the browntail moth are two serious pests species on many trees; both were introduced to North America from Europe.

Order: Lepidoptera
Family: Lymantriidae
U.S. & Canada species: 20
World species: 2,000
Wingspan: ¾–2⅓ in
(1.9–5.8 cm)

Snakeflies

Their name comes from the way they resemble a snake when they hold their heads up. The long "neck" is a feature of these insects, which are found from May to July in thickly wooded areas. A female snakefly has a long, thin ovipositor, which is easy to see. This is used to place eggs into openings in bark, and the larvae live under loose bark. Both adults and larvae are predators on aphids (see page 16) and other small, soft-bodied insects.

Order: Megaloptera—Family: Raphidiidae
U.S. & Canada species: 18—World species: 85
Body length: ¼–1⅛ in (0.6–2.8 cm)

Raphidia xanthostigma

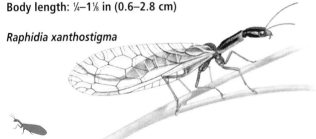

Conifer Sawflies

As in all sawflies, the ovipositor (egg-laying tube) of females in this family has evolved into a sawlike organ. With this the female cuts slits in leaves or stems and there lays her eggs. Conifer sawflies are found in conifer woods and plantations. Most species, including the European pine sawfly (*Neodiprion sertifer*, shown here), attack pine needles. A few prefer hemlock, firs, and spruce. Their larvae feed on the needles of the host tree. Through defoliation they kill or weaken the tree. The larvae pupate in a tough, brownish cocoon, either in the soil or stuck to a twig or bark crevice.

Order: Hymenoptera—Family: Diprionidae
U.S. & Canada species: 41—World species: 100
Body length: ¼–½ in (0.6–1.3 cm)

Horntails

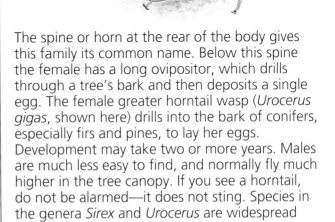

The spine or horn at the rear of the body gives this family its common name. Below this spine the female has a long ovipositor, which drills through a tree's bark and then deposits a single egg. The female greater horntail wasp (*Urocerus gigas*, shown here) drills into the bark of conifers, especially firs and pines, to lay her eggs. Development may take two or more years. Males are much less easy to find, and normally fly much higher in the tree canopy. If you see a horntail, do not be alarmed—it does not sting. Species in the genera *Sirex* and *Urocerus* are widespread across the northern hemisphere.

Order: Hymenoptera—Family: Siricidae
U.S. & Canada species: 19—World species: 100
Body length: ¾–1½ in (2–3.8 cm)

Narrow Barklice

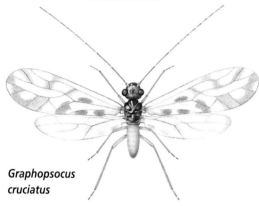

Graphopsocus
cruciatus

These are small, soft-bodied insects whose habitat is the underside of leaves, twigs, and branches of deciduous trees. Many prefer holly, box, and rhododendron. They lay their eggs in groups of 5 to 10 on stems, leaves, and fruit. These eggs are sometimes parasitized by fairyflies (see page 70). *Graphopsocus cruciatus* (shown here) is the only narrow barklouse found in North America.
Order: Psocoptera—Family: Stenopsocidae
U.S. & Canada species: 1—World species: 45
Body length: ⅟₁₆–¼ in (0.15–0.6 cm)

Cicadas

The males in this family are well known for their songs, which are easy to hear. Each species has its own song. The insects produce the songs by vibrating a pair of drumlike organs called "tymbals," one on each side of the abdomen near the thorax. The muscle attached to the tymbal contracts and relaxes very rapidly to make the song. The nymphs live underground, molt many times, and may take from 4 to 17 years to become adults because of their poor diet of root sap. The nymphs of a well-known species in North America, the periodical cicada (*Magicicada septemdecim*, shown here), construct peculiar earth chimneys above ground. In these they complete their final molt.
Order: Hemiptera
Family: Cicadidae
U.S. & Canada species: 166
World species:
2,500
Body length: 1–2 in
(2.5–5 cm)

Gall Wasps

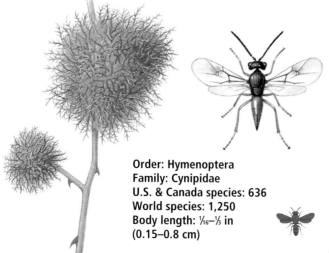

Order: Hymenoptera
Family: Cynipidae
U.S. & Canada species: 636
World species: 1,250
Body length: ⅟₁₆–⅓ in
(0.15–0.8 cm)

These small wasps lay their eggs inside plant tissue, causing the plant to produce an unusual growth called a gall. The larvae feed and grow within the gall, which protects and nourishes them. If you search in September along a hedgerow for wild roses, you will see one of the most attractive galls caused by the mossy rose gall wasp (*Diplolepis rosae*, shown here). The gall, called a robin's pincushion, is like a fluffy ball of red moss. The best place to look for other galls is on the foliage and twigs of oak trees. There you will find oak-apple galls and other strangely shaped galls.

Fireflies or Lightning bugs

An example of this family is the glow worm (*Lampyris noctiluca*, shown here). The female has no wings and emits a bright green light on the end of her body. Its purpose is to attract flying males, who flash a corresponding signal, to come and mate. Each species has its own flashing signal. The beetles are able to control the amount of oxygen supply to the special light organs, where a chemical reaction produces a yellowish or greenish light. Look for them in spring and early summer. The larvae of some species feed on snails.

Order: Coleoptera
Family: Lampyridae
U.S. & Canada
species: 200
World species: 1,900
Body length: ¼–¾ in
(0.6–2 cm)

Leaf Blotch-miner Moths

The caterpillars of these leafminer moths find a home between the upper and lower surfaces of leaves. In this small space they feed on the leaf tissue and so enlarge the space to form winding galleries, or blotchlike patches. Search for their "tracks" in leaves. You may discover the common lilac leafminer (*Caloptilia stigmatella*, shown here) in backyards, and some species are very common on oak trees. Look also for leaves which have the edges rolled; inside this kind of rainproof tent you may find some caterpillars of the family. The adults fly at dawn and dusk, and rest by day on tree trunks.

Order: Lepidoptera—Family: Gracillariidae
U.S. & Canada species: 275—World species: 1,200
Wingspan: ⅛–¾ in (0.3–2 cm)

Heleomyzid Flies

Flies in this group prefer shady, moist places, like thickets and overgrown woodland, but some have been found in mammal burrows, bird's nests, and bat caves. Their larvae generally feed on decaying plants, dung, animal corpses, fungi, and seaweeds. *Heleomyza serrata* (shown here) is a typical species. Most of the genera recorded in North America occur across the northern hemisphere. However, little is known about the biology of many species in the family.

Order: Diptera
Family: Heleomyzidae
U.S. & Canada species: 113
World species: 500
Body length: 1/16–⅓ in
(0.15–0.8 cm)

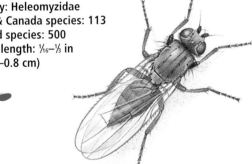

Common Scorpionflies

This insect's common name is obvious if you look at the end of the male's abdomen, which looks like a scorpion's sting. The scorpionfly has four wings instead of two, so is not a true fly. The head has a beaklike extension which is armed with biting mouthparts used to seize and eat dead or dying insects. Some species rob spider webs of freshly caught prey. Look for these insects on low-growing vegetation in shady places such as woodland margins. All the species occurring in North America belong to the genus *Panorpa*.

Order: Mecoptera
Family: Panorpidae
U.S. & Canada species: 39
World species: 360
Body length: ¾ in
(2 cm)

Scorpionfly
(*Panorpa communis*)

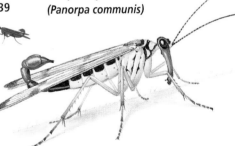

Long-horned Beetles

Search for these attractive beetles, sometimes called timber beetles, on flowers in a variety of habitats. Nocturnal species hide during the day under debris or bark. Many species are cryptically colored and others display warning colors to fend off predators. Most of them have long, narrow bodies.Their antennae are long, usually two-thirds to four times as long as the body. Their larvae burrow into timber. Some have been known to emerge from furniture made from attacked timber. The genus *Saperda* contains several species that damage apple, poplar, and maple trees.

Order: Coleoptera
Family: Cerambycidae
U.S. & Canada species: 956
World species: 25,000
Body length: ⅛–7⅛ in
(0.3–17.8 cm)

Saperda populnea

Lacebugs

These small bugs have intricate lacelike patterns. You can see these patterns better close-up with your magnifying lens. Their habitat is the underside of leaves, especially the foliage of trees and flowers in a backyard. Other species live on thistles and rhododendrons. A few species are attended by ants, while others make galls on their host plant. The females of some species guard their eggs, recognize their own young, and even lead the young nymphs from leaf to leaf.

Order: Hemiptera
Family: Tingidae
U.S. & Canada species: 157
World species: 1,820
Body length: ¹⁄₁₆–¼ in
(0.15–0.6 cm)

Dictyonota fuliginosa

Subterranean or Damp-wood Termites

Species of this family are found only in warmer regions. They make their nests in damp soil or damp timbers, and are pests because they feed on wood and can thus damage buildings. They are social insects, living in colonies of thousands of individuals, divided into workers and soldiers, each with separate functions. Despite the damage they cause, they are vital in the recycling of nutrients and an important link in ecosystems. In North America the eastern subterranean termite (*Reticulitermes flavipes*, shown here) is widespread, and is the most destructive of all termite species.

Order: Isoptera
Family: Rhinotermitidae
U.S. & Canada species: 9
World species: 200
Body length: ¼–⅓ in
(0.6–0.8 cm)

Common Barklice

If you want to find these little insects, you will have to search very thoroughly on and beneath the bark of trees, and also on twigs and branches. If you are lucky, you may encounter a herd of many hundreds, even thousands, on tree bark. They stick their eggs into crevices in the bark and cover them with a crusty layer or even "silk." There are many species still awaiting discovery and description. Members of this family are very diverse and abundant in North America.

Order: Psocoptera
Family: Psocidae
U.S. & Canada species: 62
World species: 500
Body length: ¹⁄₁₆–¼ in
(0.15–0.6 cm)

Trichadenotecnum variegatum

Carpenter & Leopard Moths

The leopard moth (*Zeuzera pyrina*, shown here) was introduced to North America from Europe. These moths live in broadleaf forests, and their larvae are found on oak, poplar, chestnut, and willow trees. The adult female lays her eggs on the bark, and the larvae feed internally in the wood. Fully grown larvae pupate in their tunnels, or in the earth in a cocoon made of silk and chewed wood fibers.
Order: Lepidoptera—Family: Cossidae
U.S. & Canada species: 45—World species: 1,000
Wingspan: ¾–3 in (2–7.5 cm)

Lappet Moths & Tent Caterpillars

The eastern tent caterpillar (*Malacosoma americana*) is a pest on apple and wild cherry trees. It is very similar to the European lackey moth (*Malacosoma neustria*, shown here). Be careful if you handle caterpillars of this family because their hairs can cause skin irritation. Some live communally in silk tents or webs spun over foliage. The fully grown caterpillars spin tough, papery, egg-shaped cocoons. You may find some of these moths flying at night, although many fly by day.
Order: Lepidoptera
Family: Lasiocampidae
U.S. & Canada species: 35
World species: 1,500
Wingspan: Up to 4 in (10 cm)

Casebearing Moths

The caterpillars of this family feed on a range of trees, shrubs, and plants in woodlands and damp meadows. As they grow, each makes itself a case from bits of its host plant, held together with silk. The adult moths lay their eggs in summer, and the caterpillars spend the winter inside their cases. Several species, such as the cigar casebearer, (*Coleophora serratella*, shown here), are pests on apple and other fruit trees, birch, larch, and other commercial trees.
Order: Lepidoptera
Family: Coleophoridae
U.S. & Canada species: 169
World species: 800
Wingspan: ¼–½ in
(0.6–1.3 cm)

Long-horned Grasshoppers

Members of this family can be found from ground level to the tree tops. They are active between dusk and dawn, when you may hear the males "singing." They are also known as katydids, because their song sounds like KATY-DID, KATY-DIDN'T. You can recognize a female by its long, sickle-shaped ovipositor (egg-laying tube). They have hearing organs on their front legs. These insects are mainly plant-feeders but some will eat other insects. Many species can be very destructive to shrubs, trees, and crop plants.

Order: Orthoptera
Family: Tettigoniidae
U.S. & Canada species: 243
World species: 5,000
Body length: ⅔–3 in
(1.6–7.5 cm)

Metrioptera roeselli

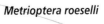

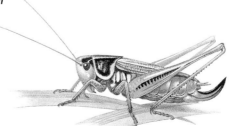

Woods & Forests

Stag Beetles

The common name for these large, shiny, black or reddish-brown insects refers to the huge jaws of the male, which look a bit like antlers. They are used for fighting during courtship. They are designed to seize the rival and flip it upside down. Their habitat is wooded areas or along sandy beaches. Some fly by night. The larvae live for up to four years in decaying tree stumps.

The stag beetle (*Lucanus cervus*) is very similar to another common North American species, the giant stag beetle (*Lucanus elaphus*).

Order: Coleoptera
Family: Lucanidae
U.S. & Canada species: 31
World species: 1,250
Body length: ¼–2½ in
(0.6–6.3 cm)

Pleasing Fungus Beetles

These small to medium-sized, oval beetles have a metallic sheen. Where tree bark is damaged and sap is flowing down the trunk, they move in to a rich source of food. Most lay eggs on fungi, and the larvae burrow deep within to feed on the fruiting bodies of the larger fungi. If you come across some fungus-infected, rotting wood, look a little closer—there may be some of this family about. Some species feed on bracket fungi, which usually grown on wood. They are a good example of how insects have adapted to a wide variety of food sources.

Order: Coleoptera
Family: Erotylidae
U.S. & Canada species: 65
World species: 2,000
Body length: ¹⁄₁₀–¾ in
(0.25–2 cm)

Dacne bipustulata

Ladybugs

Ladybugs, also called ladybirds or lady beetles, come in a variety of colors and number of spots. The background of the wing case can be black, red, yellow, or orange. The number of spots can vary from 2 to 24. Ladybugs are found in a wide range of habitats, wherever suitable food is available. The adults of most species feed on aphids and soft-bodied insects. Their larvae also eat vast numbers of aphids (see page 16). In addition to their warning colors, ladybugs produce a yellow fluid from their leg joints, which makes them taste nasty.

Order: Coleoptera
Family: Coccinellidae
U.S. & Canada species: 399
World species: 5,000
Body length: ¹⁄₁₆–⅓ in
(0.15–0.8 cm)

Two-spotted lady beetle (*Adalia bipunctata*)

Brown Lacewings

Micromus angulatus

This family of carnivorous insects is found in deciduous woodlands, backyards, and hedgerows. One brown lacewing may eat many thousands of aphids, mealy bugs, and scale insects. Brown lacewings are therefore very effective in reducing natural populations of some pests. The best time to look for them is when they become active, from dusk onward. They produce several broods a year.

Order: Neuroptera—Family: Hemerobiidae
U.S. & Canada species: 58—World species: 900
Body length: ⅛–½ in (0.3–1.3 cm)

Giant Silkworm Moths

These large, heavy-bodied moths are often brightly colored. The best examples are found in the South of the United States and in the tropics, where the largest can grow to a wingspan of 8 inches (20 centimeters). Most species have an "eyespot" near the center of each wing. The adults cannot feed because they do not have functioning mouthparts. Their caterpillars are covered in fleshy knobs that carry bristly hairs which may be tipped with irritating chemicals. The species shown, the Cynthia moth (*Samia cynthia*), was introduced to North America from Europe.

Order: Lepidoptera
Family: Saturniidae
U.S. & Canada species: 69
World species: 1,300
Wingspan: 1–6 in (2.5–15 cm)

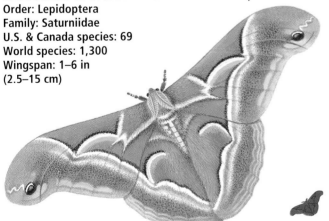

Fungus Gnats

These flies favor moist, woody areas, but they are also found in houses. Look for the long legs and humped thorax, as on the adult fungus gnat (*Mycetophila fungorum*, shown here), and on adults on the wing between March and August. The wormlike, whitish larvae of some species feed in dung, rotting wood, and other plant matter. Others feed on woody bracket fungi or fleshy fungi. In some parts of the world, cave-living species lure other small insects into silken threads. Various species are a serious pest to cultivated mushrooms.

Order: Diptera
Family: Mycetophilidae
U.S. & Canada species: 714
World species: 3,000
Body length: 1/16–½ in (0.15–1.3 cm)

Arctic, Wood Nymph, & Satyr Butterflies

These shade-loving butterflies are found in open meadows and light woodlands in upland areas. Their caterpillars all eat grass or sedges (grasslike wetland plants), and have a pair of points at the tail end. When on the wing, these butterflies may be recognized by their erratic and bobbing flight. The genus *Erebia* is typical of the mountains of North America. In fact, the majority of North American satyrid species are found in the north, or in the mountains of the West.

Order: Lepidoptera
Family: Satyridae
U.S. & Canada species: 50
World species: 2,000
Wingspan: 1⅛–3 in (2.8–7.5 cm)

Common ringlet (*Coenonympha tullia*)

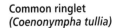

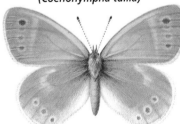

Be an Insect Detective

Once you know where to look for insects, you can become an expert by exploring different habitats. Start by looking closely at a small habitat (a microhabitat), such as a pond, a compost heap, or even a window box, to see what lives there.

Looking at leaves and stems

Garden plants often contain evidence of all kinds of insect activity. Take a look in your garden to see what you can find on the leaves and stems.

- Look carefully on a **blackberry bush** and you may find that some of the leaves are rolled up. Can you see a caterpillar inside?

- Little white lines on a **blackberry leaf** may have been caused by insects called leafminer flies (see page 15). Hold a leaf up to the light, or hold a flashlight behind it to see if you can detect the insects tunneling through it.

- If you look closely at the leaves on a **rosebush** you will probably find that some have been nibbled around the edges. This is a sign that a leafcutting bee (see page 18) has been taking away pieces of leaf to make cocoons for its eggs.

- If the **stems and buds of roses** are sticky and green, this is probably a mass of aphids (see page 16) which suck the sap inside the plant. You may also see a ladybug (see page 44) feeding on the aphids.

- **Froth on the stem of a plant** is evidence of a leafhopper (see page 16), which lives inside the bubbles that are known as "cuckoo spit." See if you can find some in your yard or a park.

- **Swellings on grass stems or leaves** may contain the larvae of flies or moths. They are called "galls." Take some home and ask an adult to open them carefully with a sharp knife. Sometimes they contain a spider, ant, or thrip that has moved into the empty gall.

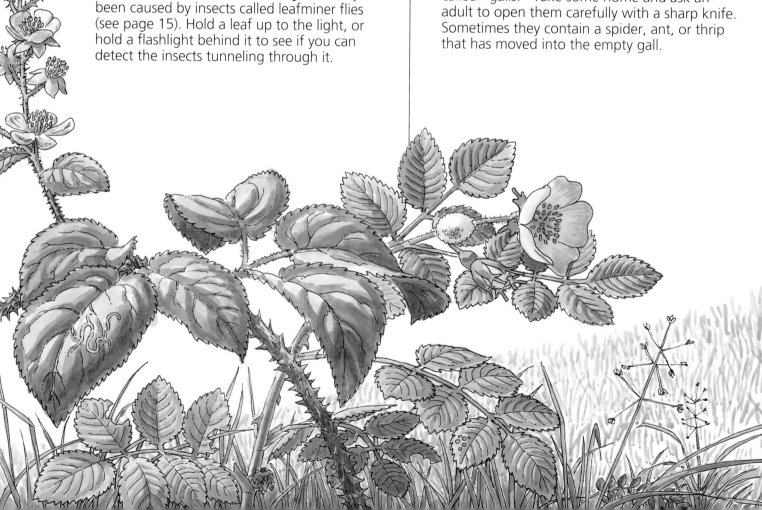

Mushroom homes

Fungi, such as mushrooms, provide homes and food for many insects. If you look at the gills under the cap of a fully grown wild mushroom or toadstool, you may see little black specks. Look with a magnifying glass and you will see that each speck is the head of a little larva. Break open the cap to see how the larvae eat tiny tunnels through it. **Always wash your hands after touching fungi; never eat wild fungi.**

A world in an oak tree

A tree such as an oak is a habitat for thousands of creatures. The leaves, fruits, and seeds are food for beetles, ants, aphids, bees, wasps, moths, and many more insects, which in turn are eaten by birds and mammals. Count how many kinds of insects you see buzzing around or crawling on a single tree. You may be surprised to discover that the tree is alive with wildlife. Make a note of the insects that you see and what they are doing.

Life inside a log

All kinds of creatures burrow into rotting wood and tree bark. If you find a rotting fallen tree or tree limb, look in the bark litter near it for insects living there.

1 **Peel away a little moss or bark** to see what is living beneath it. You may find beetles, earwigs, or even a centipede. Centipedes are not insects—they have too many legs—but they often hunt small insects.

2 **Break off part of the log** to see if there are burrowing insects. Holes and tunnels in the wood may be caused by burrowing death-watch beetle larvae (see page 38).

3 **It is always safest to observe only** rather than to touch or handle insects. Wash your hands after touching tree litter, even if you wore gloves.

Deserts & Savannas

In North America, one huge dry area extends from southern Idaho and Oregon in the United States into Mexico. A second large area extends from southern New Mexico through western Texas into Mexico. You can easily tell when you are in a desert because the ground is very dry and supports little plant life. It may rain from time to time, but never for long.

Some desert plants survive the dry conditions by storing water in their leaves, roots, or stems. The best places to look for desert insects are near plants, or around water holes.

Savannas are dry grasslands with scattered trees and only limited amounts of rain. This picture shows eight kinds of insects from this section. How many can you identify?

Ant lion, European velvet ant, digger bee, northern dune tiger beetle, robber fly, solitary wasp, spider wasp, tiphid wasp

Ant Lions

At a quick glance these large, slender-bodied insects look like damselflies (see page 55). But if you look more closely, you will see that ant lions have club-ended antennae. Search for them on dunes, and in warm, dry sandy places. They are called ant lions because the larvae prey on ants. The larvae, sometimes called doodlebugs, live in sand at the bottom of small conical pits they have dug. When an ant falls into the trap, the ant lion seizes and kills it and sucks the juices from its body.

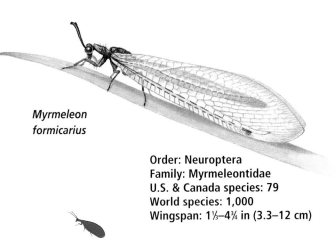

Myrmeleon formicarius

Order: Neuroptera
Family: Myrmeleontidae
U.S. & Canada species: 79
World species: 1,000
Wingspan: 1⅓–4¾ in (3.3–12 cm)

Oil or Blister Beetles

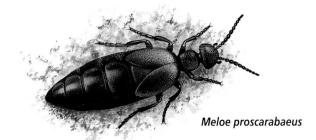

Meloe proscarabaeus

Beware! These beetles produce fluids that can raise blisters on your skin, so look but do not touch. You may see them on flowers and low-growing foliage and grass. The larvae of many species are found in the soil and eat the eggs of grasshoppers or bees. In some species, the larva attaches itself to the body of a solitary bee visiting a flower. When the female bee lays her eggs, the beetle larva sneaks into the cell with the egg. It then eats the bee's egg and the food provisions left by the parent bee for its intended offspring.

Order: Coleoptera
Family: Meloidae
U.S. & Canada species: 310
World species: 2,000
Body length: ¼–1⅓ in
(0.6–3.3 cm)

Tiger Beetles

Look for these beetles in sunny, warm, open areas, such as dry grassland and sandy places. Choose a sunny day in spring to early summer. Adult tiger beetles are fierce predators and are among the fastest insect runners. They have a top speed of 1½ mph (2.4 kilometers per hour). Their larvae dig vertical burrows, up to 11 inches (28 centimeters) deep. They wait at the top, head and jaws filling the opening, to seize any passing insect and drag it down to be eaten. If handled, both the larva and the adult beetle may give you a painful bite.

Northern dune tiger beetle
(*Cicindela hybrida*)

Order: Coleoptera
Family: Cicindelidae
U.S. & Canada species: 108
World species: 2,000
Body length: ¼–1 in
(0.6–2.5 cm)

Darkling Beetles

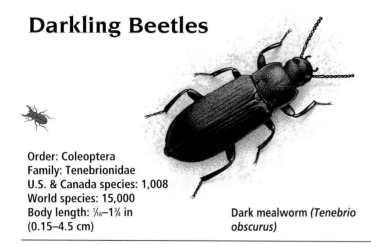

Order: Coleoptera
Family: Tenebrionidae
U.S. & Canada species: 1,008
World species: 15,000
Body length: ⅟₁₆–1¾ in
(0.15–4.5 cm)

Dark mealworm (Tenebrio obscurus)

Many species belonging to this interesting family are adapted to life in very dry conditions, such as deserts and grain storage areas. Some species produce jets of blistering chemical spray to deter their enemies, but some predatory mammals know this danger. They stick the beetle's spraying tail-end in the ground and eat them head first. Many species have very reduced hind wings, so they do not fly. Mostly, they prefer to live in dark places—hence their name. Some are called flour beetles and are pests of grains and flour.

Robber or Assassin Flies

This is a well-named family because their mouthparts are adapted for stabbing and sucking. Most species will perch on an exposed twig or stone where they keep a lookout for passing insects. If one flies near, the assassin fly chases it and seizes it on the wing with its strong, bristly legs. It quickly injects a nerve anesthetic that paralyzes the prey. Some species hunt for ground-moving prey. Many of the family mimic bees and wasps, and no insect prey is too large for them. They catch and kill dragonflies, bees, and grasshoppers, as well as other insects. They are most active in warm sunshine in open or lightly wooded areas, especially if they are dry.
Order: Diptera
Family: Asilidae
U.S. & Canada species: 883
World species: 5,500
Body length: ⅛–2 in (0.3–5 cm)

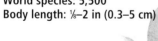

Dioctria baumhaueri

Digger, Cuckoo, & Carpenter Bees

Anthophora furcata

Digger bees dig burrows; cuckoo bees lay eggs in the nests of other bees; and carpenter bees excavate burrows in timber. They are types of solitary bees. Their habitat is widespread—they live wherever there are plenty of flowers. Cuckoo bees leave their young to feed on pollen and honey collected by their host. Digger bees collect a supply of honey and pollen and leave it in the larval cells.
Order: Hymenoptera
Family: Anthophoridae
U.S. & Canada species: 920
World species: 4,200
Body length: ⅛–1⅛ in
(0.3–2.8 cm)

Velvet Ants

The common name of this family is misleading; although these insects are velvety and some of them look like ants, they are not ants—they are wasps. The males of some species are found on flowers. The females are wingless, and are usually seen running over the ground in dry, shady, or open habitats. They are parasites on the larvae and pupae of many bees and wasps. Female velvet ants have powerful stings which cause intense pain—so don't pick them up. In North America the genus *Dasymutilla* contains species known as cow or mule killers, but they do not actually kill those animals.

Order: Hymenoptera
Family: Mutillidae
U.S. & Canada
species: 483
World species: 5,000
Body length: ⅛–1 in
(0.3–2.5 cm)

The European velvet ant (*Mutilla europaea*) prefers bumble bees as food for its larvae.

Tiphid Wasps

Adults of this family feed on flower nectar and honeydew. Females are usually seen running over the ground. They seem to prefer dry, sandy, and warm environments. All are parasites of the larvae of beetles, bees, and wasps. The antlike female of the wingless wasp (*Methocha*) will run over the ground searching for tiger beetle larvae (see page 49) in their burrows. She has to avoid the larva's powerful jaws, paralyze it, and lay her egg. She then fills in the burrow. Some species have been investigated as possible biological control agents.

Order: Hymenoptera
Family: Tiphiidae
U.S. & Canada species: 225
World species: 1,500
Body length: ⅛–1⅛ in
(0.3–2.8 cm)

Solitary Hunting, Digger, & Sand Wasps

The common names of these various sub-groups tell you their different habits. They live in sunny, sandy, open habitats. The adults feed at flowers and any source of sugary liquid. The females hunt and catch insects and spiders, which they paralyze or kill. The prey is placed in the nest, which is in the ground, in rotten wood, hollow stems, or burrows of other insects. Once the nest burrow is stocked with prey and eggs are laid, the emerging larvae will feed on the food store.

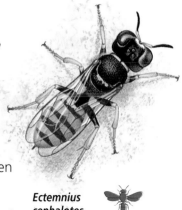

Ectemnius cephalotes

Order: Hymenoptera—Family: Sphecidae
U.S. & Canada species: 1,140—World species: 8,000
Body length: ¼–1¾ in (0.6–4.5 cm)

Spider Wasps

Adults can be seen on flowers, or running over the ground in open, dry, sandy habitats. They flick and jerk their wings continuously as they run. Their venom will paralyze even the largest spider, but the wasp has to avoid the spider's venomous fangs. If successful, the wasp lays a single egg on the paralyzed spider and buries it in the sand. A few species lay an egg on another wasp's prey. Either way, the growing larva has spider meat for a meal. **Beware of these wasps; their stings are extremely painful.**

Order: Hymenoptera
Family: Pompilidae
U.S. & Canada
species: 288
World species: 4,000
Body length: ¼–2 in
(0.6–5 cm)

Anoplius nigerrimus

Catching Insects

Check with your teacher or an expert at a local nature center before doing these activities. Nature activities can be harmful to animals or their environment, or to you, so it is always best to get expert advice and to have an adult working with you.

Remember to handle all insects gently while you observe them, then set them free afterward where you found them. Be extra careful not to trap insects that could sting you, such as wasps, bees, and hornets, and never try to catch delicate insects such as butterflies, moths, or dragonflies.

Make a beating tray

An easy way to look at insects that live on trees is to make a beating tray. **You will need:** two bamboo canes about 18 inches (45 centimeters) long, one bamboo cane 3 feet (about 1 meter) long, some white cloth (a piece of old sheet will do), strong glue or a stapler, some string or wire, and a long stick.

1 **Place one of the short canes across the top of the long cane** to make a "T" shape, and secure it tightly with some string or wire.
2 **Then lay the other short cane across the middle** of the long cane and secure it with wire or string so that it cannot move around.

Make a pitfall trap

The best way to catch crawling insects like beetles is to make a pitfall trap. **You will need:** a clean jelly jar, a trowel, a large, flat stone, and four pebbles.

1 **Choose a sheltered area of the garden** and dig a small hole in the earth, just deep and wide enough for the jelly jar.
2 **Put the jar into the hole** so that the rim is level with the ground. Make sure it doesn't wobble too much. Put a couple of leaves or a bit of grass into the jar.
3 **To keep out the rain,** place the flat stone over the top of the jar and prop it up with the pebbles.
4 **Every few hours, remove the stone** and look to see if any beetles or other crawling insects have fallen into the trap. Look at night and in the early morning, too.
5 **Remember that once an insect falls into the jar,** it cannot get out by itself, so you will have to release it. Check the trap daily.
6 **When you have finished using your pitfall trap,** remove the jar and fill in the hole.

3 **Now cut enough white cloth** to lay across the bamboo frame and overlap the edges of the top and bottom by 2 inches (5 centimeters).

4 **Lay the cloth on the ground,** then lay the frame on top. Fold the edges of the cloth over the frame and attach it with fabric glue or staples. If this is difficult, ask an adult to help you. If you glue it, don't use the tray until the glue is dry.

5 **Now find a long stick and a suitable tree**—oaks, beeches, or birches are good. Stand under the tree, holding your beating tray horizontally.

6 **Give one of the leafy branches a sharp blow with the stick.** A lot of different insects should drop on to your beating tray. You may find it easier if one person holds the tray and the other uses the stick. Be careful not to damage the tree.

Looking at water insects

Only visit a pond or stream with an adult, and approach quietly and carefully so you don't disturb the water creatures. Never run, because you could easily trip and fall in.

If you want to catch pond creatures, you will need a net. You can buy one quite cheaply, or you could make your own, using a bamboo cane with an old sieve attached to one end. You will also need a bucket filled with pond water.

1 **Push your net slowly through the water,** close to the edges and around the plants.
2 **Lift the net out of the water gently,** then empty it by dipping it into the bucket of water.
3 **Don't forget to put the insects back** into the pond after you have observed them.

Rivers & Wetlands

Rivers and wetlands play important roles in nature. Only about 3 percent of the world's water is fresh, yet it provides an amazing range of habitats.

There may be a whole world in a discarded can or tire that holds a tiny "pool" of rainwater—an ideal breeding place for gnats and mosquitoes whose larvae are aquatic. Hollows in trees and plant leaves that trap water at their bases also provide breeding sites. On a larger scale there are rain barrels, ponds, and streams.

In fast streams, only those insects with body parts for holding on to the bottom can survive. Slow-flowing streams and ponds will have a lot of interesting insects. The picture shows 12 kinds of insects from this section. How many can you identify?

Alderfly, backswimmer, diving beetle, whirligig beetles, shore bug, black fly, large caddisfly, common blue damselfly, four-spot common skimmer, pond olive, predatory stonefly, water strider

Narrow-winged Damselflies

You will find this family mainly along streams and rivers, but also around ponds, brackish pools, and swampy places. Damselflies are mostly smaller than dragonflies, and have a feeble and fluttering flight. When at rest, the wings of damselflies are held together along the body, whereas in dragonflies they are held out sideways. Female narrow-winged damselflies use their ovipositors (egg-laying tubes) to make slits in submerged plants and then insert their eggs. In some cases, the female will crawl under the surface to a depth of 12 inches (30 centimeters) or more.

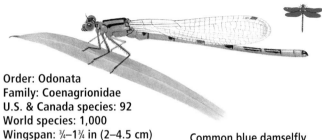

Order: Odonata
Family: Coenagrionidae
U.S. & Canada species: 92
World species: 1,000
Wingspan: ¾–1¾ in (2–4.5 cm)

Common blue damselfly
(Enallagma cyathigerum)

Spread-winged Damselflies

These relatively large damselflies are usually metallic blue, bronze, or green in color. Unlike members of other damselfly families, they rest with their wings slightly open and the body held vertical to the plant stem. On a warm, bright day between July and September you can see them sunning themselves on plants around still water, boggy areas, wet ditches, or lakes. Females lay their eggs in plant stems above water level. Larvae take about eight weeks to develop. Like all dragonfly and damselfly larvae, they have a so-called "mask" which is part of the jaw folded back under the head. They lie in wait for a small fish or other small aquatic life to come near, then shoot forward their mask and use its hooks to seize the prey.

Emerald spreadwing
(Lestes dryas)

Order: Odonata—Family: Lestidae—U.S. & Canada species: 18
World species: 200—Wingspan: 1¼–2½ in (3.1–6.3 cm)

Devil's-darning-needles or Darners

This family includes some of the largest and most powerful of the world's dragonflies. They hunt on the wing and seize many kinds of insects. Search for them in areas of still water during the midsummer months. They are inquisitive insects and investigate any moving object in their territory, including you. The aquatic nymphs, like all dragonfly nymphs, are aggressive hunters. You can catch them in your pond net if you push it through pond vegetation (see page 53).

Order: Odonata
Family: Aeshnidae
U.S. & Canada species: 34
World species: 500
Wingspan: 2⅛–4⅓ in (5.4–10.8 cm)

Subarctic darner
(Aeshna subarctica)

Common Skimmers

You will see these broad-bodied dragonflies flying over still water in a variety of habitats from dense forest to arid areas. Adult males are very territorial—they will guard their patch from a high perch on an exposed stem or twig and chase off any intruder. This is something you can watch simply by sitting quietly and observing. Eggs are laid by the female hovering over the water and dipping the tip of her abdomen below the surface. The species shown here is often found in coastal areas, but can also be found in high, hilly regions.

Order: Odonata
Family: Libellulidae
U.S. & Canada species: 91
World species: 1,250
Wingspan: ¾–4 in (2–10 cm)

Four-spot (Libellula quadrimaculata)

Black Flies

Simulium austeni

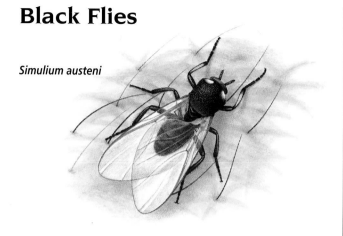

The females of some species of this family require a blood meal from birds, horses, and cattle before they lay their eggs. They have a stout body and a distinctive, humpbacked thorax. The males suck nectar. Their habitat is around fast-flowing water, where the eggs are laid on plants or stones both above and below water. The larvae feed by filtering tiny particles and organisms from the water. In cool parts of the Northern Hemisphere, they do not harm humans. However, in Africa they transmit river blindness and other parasitic diseases to humans, birds, and animals.
Order: Diptera—Family: Simuliidae—U.S. & Canada species: 143
World species: 1,500—Body length: ¹⁄₁₆–¼ in
(0.15–0.6 cm)

Mosquitoes

You will often hear these flies before you see them, for you can tell a flying mosquito by its high-pitched whine. Only the females are blood-suckers. Males, and some females also, sip nectar. When a female alights, she feels for a soft spot on the skin, then bores through it with her mouthparts and has her meal. You can find the egg rafts of mosquitoes floating on the surface of water barrels, other rain-filled containers, and ponds. Their larvae, called "wrigglers," hatch from these eggs. In tropical countries mosquitoes are carriers of many diseases, including malaria and yellow fever. In North America, mosquitoes can carry West Nile virus.
Order: Diptera
Family: Culicidae
U.S. & Canada species: 150
World species: 3,100
Body length: ⅛–¼ in
(0.3–0.6 cm)

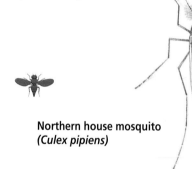

Northern house mosquito
(Culex pipiens)

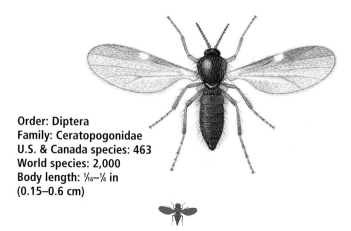

Order: Diptera
Family: Ceratopogonidae
U.S. & Canada species: 463
World species: 2,000
Body length: ¹⁄₁₆–¼ in
(0.15–0.6 cm)

Biting Midges or Punkies

Because of their small size, biting midges are often called "no-see-'ums." But you will certainly feel the effect of their biting and blood-sucking, especially near sunset. Most species do not fly more than 100 yards (91 meters) from their breeding ground in moist habitats such as bogs, pond margins, rivers, lakes, and close to the seashore. Some species, like *Forcipomyia bipunctata* (shown here), suck the body fluids of larger insects such as dragonflies, moths, and beetles; others catch and eat smaller insects.

The Ephemeroptera are the oldest group of winged insects on Earth today. The name of the order comes from two Greek words: *ephemeros* (lasting a day) and *pteron* (wing) because the adults usually live for about a day.

Burrowing Mayflies

Look for the adult mayflies from mid-April to September when you may see vast numbers flying above a river or stream. The front legs of their nymphs are adapted for digging. They burrow into sand or silt at the bottom of streams, rivers, lakes, or ponds. Their specially adapted mouthparts move the silt, which is then pushed backward by the legs. Members of this family are important links in the freshwater-fish food chains. *Ephemera danica* (shown here) is among the largest of North American mayflies. Anglers use models of it as lures, and it is known as a "green drake."

Order: Ephemeroptera
Family: Ephemeridae
U.S. & Canada species: 13
World species: 150
Body length: ½–1¼ in
(1.3–3.1 cm)

Prongill Mayflies

One way to distinguish members of this family from other mayflies is by the length of their three long tails. In prongill mayflies, they are obviously longer than the body. Their habitat is slow-flowing streams and lakes. The nymphs prefer to live in crevices under stones and logs, or in plant debris. They eat plants and the debris. These nymphs are freely eaten by fish and thus form an important link in the food chain.

Order: Ephemeroptera
Family: Leptophlebiidae
U.S. & Canada species: 70
World species: 600—Body length:
⅛–½ in (0.3–1.3 cm)

Sepia dun (*Leptophlebia marginata*)

Small Mayflies

To find the nymphs of these beautiful mayflies, try pond-dipping (see page 53) in their habitat, which is streams, rivers, ditches, ponds, or lakes. If you keep some specimens in your aquarium, be sure to plant it with a variety of aquatic plants because the nymphs are herbivorous (plant-eating). The pond olive (*Cloeon dipterum*, shown here) gives birth to live nymphs and does not lay eggs. Other species of small mayflies will enter water or even go through waterfalls to lay their eggs on rocks. Some species can live in polluted water, which is unusual for most insects.

Order: Ephemeroptera
Family: Baetidae
U.S. & Canada species: 147
World species: 800
Body length: ¹⁄₁₆–½ in
(0.15–1.3 cm)

Stream Mayflies

Try pond-dipping (see page 53) for the nymphs of these mayflies in fast-running mountain streams. If you catch one, observe it in some water in a plastic dish, then return it to its habitat. They are difficult to keep in an aquarium because they are used to cold, fast-running water rich in oxygen. Because they are an important freshwater fish food, anglers use models of both nymphs and adults as lures for fly fishing. The nymphs of many species are active and can move easily in all directions.

Order: Ephemeroptera
Family: Heptageniidae
U.S. & Canada species: 133
World species: 550
Body length: ⅛–½ in (0.3–1.3 cm)
Olive upright dun
(*Rhithrogena semicolorata*)

Predatory Stoneflies

Some adult species of this family have no working mouthparts, so they live for less than two weeks using the food reserves within their bodies. Other species may feed on pollen. In contrast, their nymphs are carnivorous (meat-eating) or omnivorous (they eat everything). When fully grown, they crawl out of the water, rest on a stone, and complete the transformation to their adult state. They are found near cold, stony, and gravel-bottomed streams; some species live in water rich in limestone. The best time to look for the day-flying adults is from late spring to early summer. Most species are found in the North and West, but they are not common.

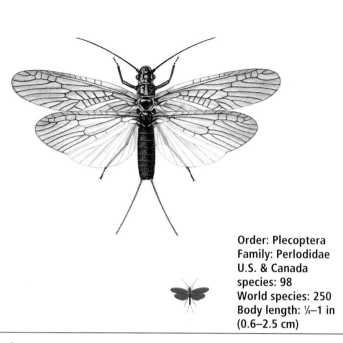

Order: Plecoptera
Family: Perlodidae
U.S. & Canada
species: 98
World species: 250
Body length: ¼–1 in
(0.6–2.5 cm)

Spring or Brown Stoneflies

Nymphs in this family may pass through 30 molts and take four years to become adults. Their eggs may be flattened or spindle-shaped; they may be adhesive or have a threadlike attachment to stick to underwater objects. You should search for them in fast-flowing rocky streams. They are weak fliers, usually seen in warm sunshine. Many species avoid polluted water and prefer cold, oxygen-rich water. The vast majority of the American species belong to the genus *Nemoura* (one is shown here). Members of this family are used as models for the anglers' flies called "early brown."

Order: Plecoptera
Family: Nemouridae
U.S. & Canada
species: 58
World species: 400
Body length: ¼–½ in
(0.6–1.3 cm)

Stonefly
(*Nemoura cinerea*)

Rolled-winged Stoneflies

Some species of this family are called needleflies because of their small size and slender shape. When at rest, the wings appear to be tightly rolled together over the sides of the body. Their favored habitat is small streams and springs, but they are also found beside lakes in lowlands and uplands. *Leictra geniculata* (shown here) belongs to the largest genus in this family, which is found throughout the Northern Hemisphere.

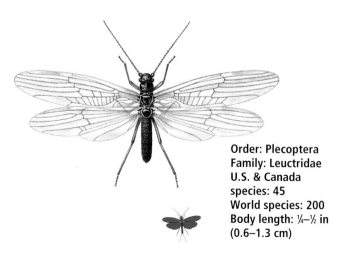

Order: Plecoptera
Family: Leuctridae
U.S. & Canada
species: 45
World species: 200
Body length: ¼–½ in
(0.6–1.3 cm)

Non-biting Midges

This is a family of gnatlike flies that look a little like mosquitoes. Look for them between April and September over trees, bushes, or water. You will often see swarms of them toward dusk "dancing" up and down in still air, and the females mating before they lay eggs on the water surface. Most of their three-year life cycle is spent underwater as larvae—the adults only live a week or two. The larvae of some species of this family are often called bloodworms because of their red color. A few species lives on the seashore, and some even live in thermal springs.

Order: Diptera
Family: Chironomidae
U.S. & Canada species: 670
World species: 2,000
Body length: ¹⁄₁₆–⅓ in
(0.15–0.8 cm)

Buzzer midge
(Chironomus plumosus)

Micro Caddisflies

The smallest species of caddisflies belongs to this family. Their habitat is near rivers, lakes, and ponds. Mating swarms fly over the water and lay jellylike egg masses both on the water and marginal plants. The first of four larval stages move freely in the water, sucking the juices of water plants. The last larval age produces silk from its mouthparts and weaves an open-ended barrel-shaped case. The larva pupates inside this case and emerges at the water surface.

Order: Trichoptera
Family: Hydroptilidae
U.S. & Canada species: 200
World species: 1,000
Body length: ¹⁄₁₆–¼ in
(0.15–0.6 cm)

Agraylea multipunctata

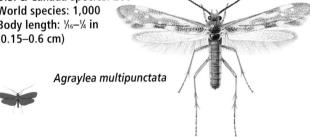

Northern Caddisflies

Limnephilus rhombicus

Search for these common caddisflies around ponds, lakes, and still water. *Limnephilus rhombicus*, a typical adult caddisfly, is a member of a widespread genus of more than 311 species in North America. These species and their larvae live in cases made from tiny pieces of plant stem, stones, sand grains, and small snail shells. Some species make cases from small twigs and these are known as log cabins. Use your pond net gently and push it through the underwater plants to catch the larvae.

Order: Trichoptera—Family: Limnephilidae
U.S. & Canada species: 311—World species: 1,500
Body length: ¼–1¼ in (0.6–3.1 cm)

Large Caddisflies

Wings of adults of some members of this species can be brightly marked with orange and black. You will find them near ponds, lakes, marshes, and slow-moving parts of streams, and rivers. The larvae make beautiful, regular, tapering cases of spirally arranged plant fragments. The pieces of plant fragment used are cut to an exact size as the larvae measures them against the front part of its body. Some cases can be up to nearly 2½ inches (6.3 centimeters) long.

Order: Trichoptera
Family: Phryganeidae
U.S. & Canada species: 26
World species: 500
Body length: ½–1 in
(1.3–2.5 cm)

Agrypnia pagetana

Stilt Bugs

These bugs get their names from the way they walk with their bodies held high on spindly legs. Slow-moving, they "freeze" if disturbed. Because of their secretive habits they are difficult to find. Their habitat is among tall grasses and weeds in woodlands, meadows, and by the margins of ponds. *Berytinus minor* (shown here) use their protective coloring to help them blend into their surroundings. Although most are herbivores (plant-eaters), some species can be partly predaceous, feeding on insect eggs and small, soft-bodied prey. In North America some species may have three or four generations a year.

Order: Hemiptera—Family: Berytidae
U.S. & Canada species: 14
World species: 180
Body length: ¼–⅓ in (0.6–0.8 cm)

Pygmy Grasshoppers

These insects are common in some areas. Their habitat is moist woodlands and the margins of bogs and lakes. They eat grasses, mosses, and lichens. Unlike many species in this order, their courtship is silent. The male bows in front of the female and vibrates his wings. Members of this family do not stridulate (make the typical cricket sound) and have no hearing organs. Many species have gray or brown camouflage to match the mossy or stony ground where they live. There is still a great deal to be learned about their lifestyles.

Order: Orthoptera
Family: Tetrigidae
U.S. & Canada species: 29
World species: 1,000
Body length: ¼–¾ in (0.6–2 cm)

Granulated grouse locust (Tetrix subulata)

Alderflies

If you search for these in May and June, you will find these insects at rest on alder trees and similar waterside vegetation. They are lazy fliers, so you should be able to take a close look at one without disturbing it. A female may lay many hundreds of eggs in clusters on waterside plants. The young larvae crawl into the water and live there for nearly two years. When fully grown, the larvae crawl out of the water and pupate on the land.

Order: Megaloptera—Family: Sialidae
U.S. & Canada species: 23—World species: 75
Body length: ⅓–¾ in (0.8–2 cm)

Sialis lutaria

Mole Crickets

These generally reddish-brown insects are adapted to subterranean life (underground). They are not true crickets. The front legs are modified for digging. Their eyes are small and their wings are leathery, covering only half the abdomen. From the front they look like tiny moles. They live in sand or soil near streams, ponds, or lakes, and their burrows can go nearly 8 inches (20 centimeters) belowground. They build elaborate "singing burrows" with a special shape, which increases the volume of their song. On a still night they can be heard up to almost a mile (or 1.6 kilometers) away.

Order: Orthoptera—Family: Gryllotalpidae
U.S. & Canada species: 7—World species: 60
Body length: ¾–1¾ in (2–4.5 cm)

European mole cricket (Gryllotalpa gryllotalpa)

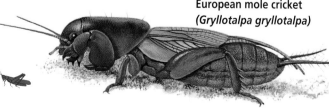

Shore Bugs

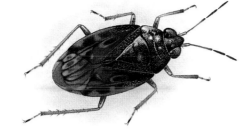

Saldula pallipes

As their name suggests, shore bugs are found around the margins of the seashore among seaweed, salt marshes, grasses, mosses, and low vegetation. These species can survive being submerged by the tide. Many, however, may be found in streams, ponds, ditches, and similar places. They are difficult to see, because they hide in holes and rock crevices. These bugs can run, jump, and fly, or burrow into mud, where some spend part of their life cycle. As far as is known, all members of this family are predaceous (they hunt other creatures for food).
Order: Hemiptera—Family: Saldidae—U.S. & Canada species: 76
World species: 300—Body length: ⅛–¼ in (0.3–0.6 cm)

Shore Flies

Psilopa compta

This family is found in many types of wetlands, such as marshes, wet meadows, pool margins, lakes, rivers, and the seashore. Their larvae are either semi-aquatic or aquatic. They feed on sewage and carrion; some mine into meadow grasses, and others live in the stems of water plants. While most shore flies prefer fresh water, some can tolerate very salty water. You may find a cluster of them on the surface of a pool above the high tidemark. One unusual species can breed in pools of crude oil! A few of these flies have front legs like those of praying mantises (see page 32), which they use to capture small insects.
Order: Diptera—Family: Ephydridae—U.S. & Canada species: 426
World species: 1,400—Body length: ⅛–½ in (0.3–1.3 cm)

Long-legged Flies

Dolichopus ungulatus

These flies will be found in wet habitats, such as marshy places, the edges of streams and lakes, meadows, and woodlands. A few species live on the seashore. The adults seize small insects, which they crush and chew before sucking up the juices. Look for these flies during the summer months. A great deal remains to be discovered about many of their larval ways of life. In the way that birds use parts of their body to signal to mates, these flies do the same. The males have hairy tufts and other "decoration" on their legs, which they show off to the females. When watching insects, always remember to keep your eyes open for aspects of their behavior.
Order: Diptera—Family: Dolichopodidae
U.S. & Canada species: 1,227
World species: 5,500
Body length: Most under ⅛ in (0.3 cm)

Striped Earwigs

You can search for these nocturnal earwigs under debris, especially on seashores, mudflats, and the banks of rivers, but you will be lucky to find one because they are not very common. The riparian earwig (*Labidura riparia*, shown here) is the only one in this family to occur in North America. It prefers sandy habitats where it can dig deep tunnels in which to lay its eggs. Do not handle these earwigs because they will try to give you a pinch with their forceps. Some species can also discharge a smelly liquid over a short distance.
Order: Dermaptera
Family: Labiduridae
U.S. & Canada species: 1
World species: 75
Body length:
Up to 1⅓ in (3.3 cm)

Marsh Treaders

This is a family of very slender, reddish to dark brown bugs. The genus *Hydrometra* is the most common in North America. They are found on quiet pools, marshes, swamps, stagnant and even brackish water. Their bodies and legs are well covered with fine hairs that repel water. They walk slowly on the surface near the water's edge. They skewer small insect larvae and other small water creatures on their tubelike mouthparts. The female lays her eggs singly and sticks them to plants at the edge of the water, or to objects at water level. Search for them in June and July, when new adults hatch from the eggs.

Order: Hemiptera
Family: Hydrometridae
U.S. & Canada species: 9
World species: 110
Body length: ½–¾ in (1.3–2 cm)

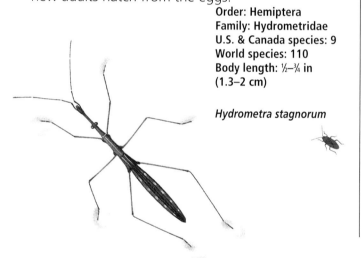

Hydrometra stagnorum

Backswimmers

Although they look a little like water boatmen (see opposite page), the backswimmers—as their name suggests—swim on their backs. Their long hind legs are fringed with hairs and used as oars. Strong swimmers, they can leap into the air through the water's surface film and fly away. They rest at the surface. They are underwater predators feeding on insects, small fish, tadpoles— and even fingers if given the chance! Males can make sounds to attract females by rasping their mouthparts on their front legs.

Order: Hemiptera
Family: Notonectidae
U.S. & Canada species: 35
World species: 300
Body length: ¹⁄₁₆–⅔ in (0.15–1.6 cm)

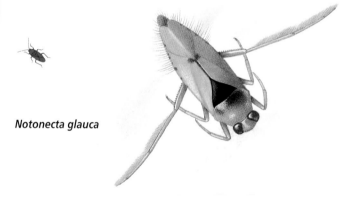

Notonecta glauca

Water Striders

In this family, the feet and underside of the body have a dense covering of water-repellent hairs. This enables these insects literally to walk on the water's surface. Their legs also have ripple-sensitive hairs, so if you tap the water's surface, you will see them react. Look for these interesting insects on still or slow-running water. Most species have winged, short-winged, and wingless forms. The ones with wings can fly off to new areas and start new populations.

Order: Hemiptera
Family: Gerridae
U.S. & Canada species: 45
World species: 500
Body length: ¹⁄₁₆–¼ in (0.15)–0.6 cm)

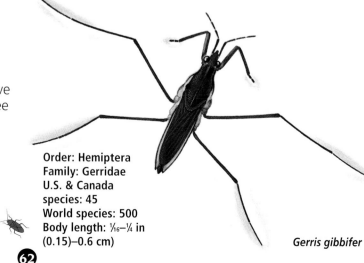

Gerris gibbifer

Water Boatmen

These are interesting insects that can swim rapidly and which carry their air supply as a bubble in a reservoir under their wings. This makes them buoyant, so they have to hang on to plants in order to remain in deeper water. Some species are predacious on other aquatic insects and even fish. Some species are unique among bugs because they can eat minute particles of solid food. All other bugs (hemiptera) suck up liquid food. Corixids can fly well and are attracted to lights at night.

Order: Hemiptera
Family: Corixidae
U.S. & Canada species: 122
World species: 525
Body length: ⅛–½ in (0.3–1.3 cm)

Glaenocorisa propinqua

Water Scorpions

Water scorpions lie in wait, hidden among vegetation, to ambush their prey. Their powerful front legs (known as raptorial legs) seize tadpoles, mosquito larvae, and most other small water creatures. Having seized their prey, they suck out the body juices. They thrust their long breathing tube out through the surface film to renew their air supply. Although they are fully winged, they seldom fly. You might be lucky and catch one if you push your pond net slowly through the water weeds in slow-moving or still water. However, be careful—they can give you a painful bite if touched.

Order: Hemiptera
Family: Nepidae
U.S. & Canada species: 13
World species: 200
Body length: ½–1¾ in (1.3–4.5 cm)

Nepa cinera

Predaceous Diving Beetles

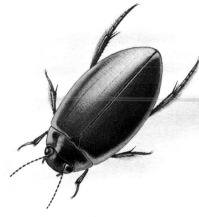

Most diving beetles carry a supply of air enclosed in their wing cases. They renew it by projecting their tail ends into the air. Their habitats vary from streams, ditches, canals, and lakes to ponds. If the habitat

Colymbetes fuscus

dries up, the beetles fly away to a new site. Both adults and larvae are predators on small fish, frogs, newts, snails, and many other kinds of water life. They suck out the body contents after injecting a digestive substance into their prey. When you go pond-dipping (see page 53), you will almost certainly capture some.

Order: Coleoptera—Family: Dytiscidae
U.S. & Canada species: 475—World species: 3,500
Body length: ¹⁄₁₆–1⅓ in (0.15–3.3 cm)

Whirligig Beetles

Look for groups of these beetles on the surface of slow-moving water and ponds. If you gently tap the water surface, you will see them react by diving because their antennae are sensitive to ripples. Although adapted for water life, they can fly well. Their blue-black, highly polished, and streamlined upper body surfaces are waterproof. They use their middle and hind pairs of legs as oars and the front pair to seize mosquito larvae and dead insects floating on the surface.

Order: Coleoptera
Family: Gyrinidae
U.S. & Canada species: 58
World species: 750
Body length: ¹⁄₁₆–⅔ in (.15–1.6 cm)

Gyrinus minutus

Keeping Insects at Home

Have you ever thought of having your own insect zoo at home? Many kinds of insects are easy to keep, and it is great fun watching their behavior close-up. However, get your parents' permission first. You should only collect insects to observe them. Don't keep them more than 2 to 3 days, and always release them back into the habitat where you caught them.

The rules for success are:
1 **Always handle insects very gently**—their legs and wings are often delicate.
2 **Keep the cage away from direct sunlight** and away from direct heat.
3 **Provide small air holes in the lid** or use fine netting. Insects breathe just as other animals do.
4 **Provide fresh food daily** and remove all uneaten food at the same time.
5 **Clean out the cages** after you release one group of insects and before you put in another.

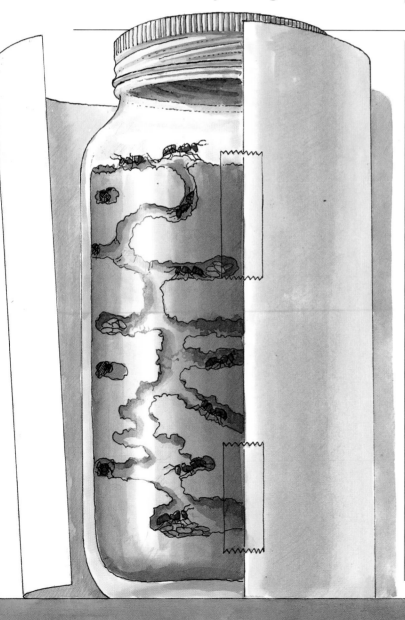

Insect cages

The best cages for insect watching are large jelly jars or preserving jars. If you are using the metal screw-on top as its lid, ask an adult to punch 6 to 8 small air holes into it. Or you can stretch a piece of fine material, like nylon or muslin, over the top and attach it with a strong rubber band. Always put some leaves and a twig in the bottom of the jar so that the insects have some shelter. For a larger cage, like a fish tank, bend a wire coat hanger into a rough rectangle and attach the material to it with staples. Weight the corners to prevent escapes.

Ant nest

You can easily make an ant home from a large glass jar. Partly fill it with soil and cover the outside with lightproof paper. Fasten it to the jar with adhesive tape. Cover the container with fine material as described above.
1 **Dig up an ant nest** in your yard and try to find the biggest ant (a queen). Wear gloves because the worker ants will try to defend her.
2 **Put the queen in her new home** with as many workers as you can collect.
3 **Feed the ants every day** with a little sugar or honey sprinkled on the soil surface.
4 **In time they will excavate tunnels against the glass**. Remove the paper around the jar from time to time to see how they are doing.

Mini vivarium

You can make a wonderful, ever-changing habitat in an old fish tank or large plastic candy jar. By adding stones, dead leaves, a clump of grass, and soil or sand, you can make a home for beetles and grasshoppers. A long-horned grasshopper (see page 43) will live well in a grassy tank with some branches for it to crawl on. If you have two grasshoppers, you may hear them singing after dark. Always release them after a few days.

Earwig nest

Earwigs (see page 10) will live quite comfortably in a plastic kitchen storage box. Put moist—not wet—soil in the box with a couple of flat stones or a piece of bark for them to hide under. Add some ground litter in one corner. If you keep some earwigs between January and March, they may lay their eggs. They will need tiny pieces of raw meat and bits of lettuce, cucumber, or a slice of apple as food.

What's inside?

Many different insects make galls. Why not collect and hatch them? In spring, gall wasps (see page 40) lay their eggs on the buds of oak trees, which causes brown, marblelike galls to form. Inside the galls, the wasp larvae are growing, and in the fall, the adult wasps will eat their way out and fly off.

1 **Look for galls** on the ground in woods, on oaks and many other plants and trees. Collect them in late summer and fall.
2 **Cut the twig or plant stem** so that it fits into a jelly jar.
3 **Make holes in the lid or cover the container** as described on the preceding page.
4 **Put the jars in your garage**, tool shed, or on a balcony for the winter.
5 **In the spring, watch** for the tiny adult insects to emerge. Be sure to release the full-grown insects.

Pests & Parasites

These include insects that are pests of humans, their belongings, buildings, livestock, and crops. A lot is known about parasites and the insect pests whose attacks cause commercial damage. But the enemies of most insect species are, as yet, unknown.

Parasites are organisms that live on and eat the tissues of their living host. They do not necessarily kill their hosts, although many do. In general, an insect parasite uses one host animal in or on which to carry out its complete development from egg to adult. The eggs may be laid on or in the host, and the hatching larvae feed on the host's body tissues or fluids. If they do this on the surface of the host's body (like bed bugs), they are called "ectoparasites." If they do it from within, they are called "endoparasites." Some parasites live on or in a particular animal—such as feather lice, which live on birds—while others live in a particular animal's home.

Some parasites live permanently in peoples' houses, while others stay for short periods only. All are attracted by materials found in houses that parasites use for food.

Most pests attack a specific crop—they can range from the annoying, like the black fly on a rose tree, to life-threatening, like the plagues of locusts that sweep across Africa, eating everything in their path. This picture shows 11 kinds of insects from this section. How many can you identify?

Varied carpet beetle, sheep botfly, head louse, silverfish, encyrtid wasp, mealy bugs, ichneumon wasp, cowpea weevil, greenhouse whitefly, German cockroach, cuckoo wasp

Pests & Parasites

Chewing Lice

This family of tiny, wingless, parasitic lice have special claws adapted to hold on to their host's feathers. The poultry shaft louse (*Menopon gallinae*, shown here) gives you a good idea of a typical family member. You are more likely to see their effect than to find the lice, unless you look very closely. The female attaches eggs singly to feathers with a waterproof, gluelike substance. The larvae then feed by scraping off the skin and feathers, which causes the bird to become bald in places and become unhealthy.

Order: Phthiraptera
Family: Menoponidae
U.S. & Canada species: 260
World species: 650
Body length: ¹⁄₁₆–¼ in (0.15–0.6 cm)

Human Lice

The eggs of this small family are commonly known as "nits." The adults have curved legs, each armed with a large claw for grasping hair. There is one species that lives on humans, but there are two distinct sub-species: the body louse (*Pediculus humanus corporis*) and the head louse (*Pediculus humanus capitis*, shown here). The former lives in clothing, laying its eggs along the seams, but leaves to feed on human blood before hiding again. It carries typhus and other fevers. The head louse lives entirely in the hair and passes from host to host by headwear, combs, brushes, and direct contact.

Order: Phthiraptera
Family: Pediculidae
U.S. & Canada species: 1
World species: 2
Body length: ¹⁄₁₆–⅛ in (0.15–0.3 cm)

Mammal-chewing Lice

These small lice live in the micro-habitat provided by the hair or fur of their host mammal. Since they are always in very close contact with their host within a very small microhabitat, they do not need sight, so they have evolved as eyeless, or almost eyeless, insects. Some, like the dog louse (*Trichodectes canis,* shown here) are pests on domestic animals. This louse often transmits tapeworms from dog to dog. As they feed on skin, hair, fur, and blood, they cause great irritation to their hosts.

Order: Phthiraptera
Family: Trichodectidae
U.S. & Canada species: 137
World species: 350
Body length: ¹⁄₁₆–⅛ in (0.15–0.3 cm)

Common Fleas

The family of common fleas is ideally adapted to its habitats, which are the bodies of mammals and birds. The mouthparts are modified to pierce skin and suck blood. Fleas have narrow bodies, perfect for moving about between hairs. Their legs are long and strong, and they have a special structure built into the thorax, which acts as an energy store, and makes fleas great jumpers. The structure acts like a bow firing an arrow. The cat flea (*Ctenocephalides felis*, shown here) can high-jump around 100 times its own body length—about 13 inches (33 centimeters). A single cat can support a very large population of fleas. Females lay their eggs on the ground and the larvae emerge. When they change to pupae, they can remain like that for years until a suitable host comes along.

Order: Siphonaptera
Family: Pulicidae
U.S. & Canada species: 16
World species: 200
Body length: ¹⁄₁₆–⅓ in (0.15–0.8 cm)

Flesh Flies

These flies live in a variety of habitats, where they are able to feed on flower nectar, aphids' honeydew, or sap flowing from tree wounds. The adult females give birth to larvae and do not lay eggs. The food of species in the family varies: many feed on carrion (dead and rotting flesh). Some are parasites on beetles, grasshoppers, and caterpillars of moths and butterflies, and some parasitize turtles and frogs. They look a little like blow flies (see page 14) but are striped dull gray and black; they are never metallic. Some species are used to control insect pests.

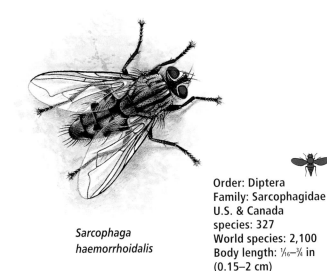

Sarcophaga haemorrhoidalis

Order: Diptera
Family: Sarcophagidae
U.S. & Canada species: 327
World species: 2,100
Body length: 1/16–3/4 in (0.15–2 cm)

Botflies & Warble Flies

The flies in this family are very heavy-bodied and look a little like honey or bumble bees. They often have hairy abdomens. The sheep botfly (*Oestrus ovis*, shown here) gives you a good idea of their appearance. Their habitat tends to be close to their host species. In some species the males gather on hilltops for mating purposes.

Warble flies fasten their eggs firmly to hairs on the legs of a cow, and the larvae burrow under the skin all the way to the animal's back. When mature, they chew their way out, leaving a terrible sore, and pupate in the soil.

Order: Diptera
Sheep botfly family: Oestridae
Warble fly family: Hypodermatidae
U.S. & Canada species: 41
World species: 160
Body length: 1/3–1 in (0.8–2.5 cm)

Louse Flies

These strange-looking flies live as parasites, sucking blood from the bodies of birds or mammals, including deer, cattle, sheep, and horses. They have long, curved claws, which hold on to the fur or feathers of their active and moving habitat, and short antennae. As wings and eyes are not needed for their way of life, many species of the family have lost them. The female lays fully grown larvae, which have grown inside her body feeding on special "milk glands." The mature larvae of the sheep ked (*Melophagus ovinus*, shown here) attach themselves to the sheep's wool by using a special sticky substance they produce before pupating.

Order: Diptera
Family: Hippoboscidae
U.S. & Canada species: 28
World species: 200
Body length: 1/16–1/2 in (0.15–1.3 cm)

Pests & Parasites

Stylopids

These small parasites are seldom seen because of their way of life. The males look a bit like beetles. The females are grublike and live on their hosts, especially andrenid bees, sand wasps, and the social wasps (see pages 18, 19, and 51). Their larvae crawl into flowers, where they wait to hitch a ride on a suitable host. Once aboard, they bore into the body and feed on its internal organs without killing the host. After pupation in the host's body, the males fly away, but the females remain, with the tip of the body sticking out as shown here. The odor they give off attracts males to mate with them.

Order: Strepsiptera
Family: Stylopidae
U.S. & Canada species: 80
World species: 260
**Body length: 1/16–1/8 in
(0.15–0.3 cm)**

Stylops melittae

Bee Flies

You should look for these hairy, beelike flies on a sunny day. They can often be seen flying, hovering, and sucking nectar from celandines and other early spring flowers. Do not worry about their beelike buzzing—they have no stinger. They lay eggs in the burrows of solitary bees and wasps; their larvae are parasitic on them, as well as beetles, moths, and grasshoppers. The pupae have sharp teeth at one end, which break open the seal of the host cell so that the adult fly may escape.

Order: Diptera
Family: Bombyliidae
**U.S. & Canada
species: 797**
World species: 5,000
**Body length: 1/16–1 in
(0.15–2.5 cm)**

**Black-tailed bee fly
(*Bombylius major*)**

Tachinid Flies

Most of these look like bristly houseflies (see page 15), but some are much larger, very hairy, and look like bees. They can be found in many habitats drinking nectar, tree sap, or honeydew (the secretion from aphids), but they are hard to catch. Males of many species gather on hilltops waiting for females to fly near so that they can mate. All their larvae are parasitic upon other insects; the adults lay their eggs on or inside the hosts, which may be butterflies, beetles, bees, wasps, bugs, or flies. Parasitic flies are such efficient controllers of certain insect pests that many are used as biological control agents.

Voria ruralis

Order: Diptera—Family: Tachinidae
U.S. & Canada species: 1,277—World species: 7,800
Body length: 1/16–1/2 in (0.15–1.3 cm)

Fairyflies

This family of tiny wasps contains some of the smallest insects on Earth. The females lay their eggs inside the eggs of dragonflies, grasshoppers, butterflies and moths, beetles, and flies. One species, *Caraphractus cinctus* (shown here), uses its wings to swim through the water to reach the submerged eggs of giant water beetles. They can remain underwater for days at a time. Try to imagine how insects this small can search for and find the eggs they are going to parasitize.

Order: Hymenoptera
Family: Mymaridae
U.S. & Canada species: 120
World species: 1,300
**Body length: 1/16–1/8 in
(0.15–0.3 cm)**

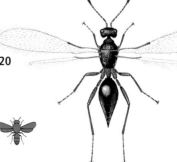

Braconid Wasps

Brown, reddish-brown, or black, these wasps have quite slender bodies. They parasitize other insects. *Apanteles glomeratus* (shown here) searches out the larvae of the cabbage white butterfly to lay its eggs in them. The wasp larvae then feed on the body of the host. Finally, some 30 or more larvae emerge and spin yellowish, silken cocoons on the outside of the host's body. Search for these "parasitized" caterpillars on cabbage leaves and other foliage, or on the walls of sheds and buildings. Leaving cabbage butterfly caterpillars in small tubes over the winter may also provide you with some parasitic wasps or flies. Many species from this family are used as biological control agents.

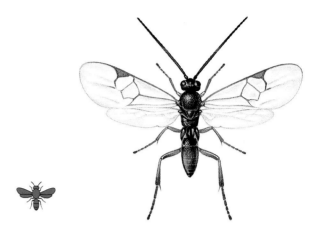

Order: Hymenoptera
Family: Braconidae
U.S. & Canada species: 2,000
World species: 15,000
Body length: 1/16–1/2 in (0.15–1.3 cm)

Encyrtid Wasps

The majority of these wasps are found in the same environments as their hosts, which can be scale insects, mealy bugs, aphids, and whiteflies. The wasps lay their eggs in the bodies of both immature and adult stages. Some of them lay eggs that divide repeatedly at a very early stage in their growth to produce between 10 and 2,000 larvae from a single egg. Others parasitize the larvae of braconid wasps, which are already living as parasites in another larva. *Habrolepis dalmanni* (shown here) is used to control a scale insect that damages oak trees, and other species have been used to control citrus pests.

Order: Hymenoptera—Family: Encyrtidae
U.S. & Canada species: 509
World species: 3,000
Body length: 1/16–1/8 in (0.15–0.3 cm)

Cuckoo Wasps

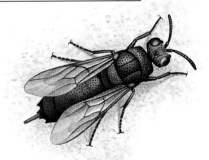

Chrysis fuscipennis often rolls itself into a ball as a protection against predators.

The body of the cuckoo wasp can be bright blue, green, red, copper, or mixed patterns, all with a shiny, metallic hue. This is how they get their other name: jewel wasps. On a hot, sunny day look along fences, sheltered walls, or banks where solitary bees and wasps may be living.

They are parasites, searching for larval burrows in which to lay their eggs. However, the larvae do not always eat their host, which the female had paralyzed, but eat its food supply instead. Some species parasitize sawfly larvae (see page 19), and a few eat praying mantis eggs (see page 32).

Order: Hymenoptera—Family: Chrysididae
U.S. & Canada species: 227—World species: 3,000
Body length: 1/8–3/4 in (0.3–2 cm)

Eulophid Wasps

These very tiny wasps are able to find many kinds of hidden larvae, like the leaf-blotch miner moths' larvae (see page 41). They kill these larvae by laying eggs in their bodies. The wasps are an important link in the chain of life because they help to control natural insect populations, such as those of moths, beetles, aphids, and scale insects. Today some species are bred and released into the environment to help control insect pests of larch and pine trees.

Baryscapus bruchophagi

Order: Hymenoptera—Family: Eulophidae
U.S. & Canada species: 507
World species: 3,100
Body length: ¹⁄₁₆–¼ in (0.15–0.6 cm)

Pteromalid Wasps

All known pteromalid wasps are either black or a very metallic blue or green. Being parasitic, they are found everywhere that their host species live. A few form galls, while some are herbivores or hunt small insects, such as the larvae of the gall midge or the eggs of other insect species. The larvae of one world species destroy houseflies and related insects, while another attacks fleas. These wasps are good examples of the useful work carried on by a tiny insect, which very few of us have ever seen. There are still many undescribed species.

Order: Hymenoptera
Family: Pteromalidae
U.S. & Canada species: 395
World species: 3,200
Body length: ¹⁄₁₆–⅓ in (0.15–0.8 cm)

Pteromalus dolichurus

Ichneumon Wasps

If you see a long, narrow-bodied insect waving its antennae as it crawls about on a flat-topped flower, you may have found an ichneumon wasp. Most of the females have an ovipositor (long egg-laying tube). The picture shows *Rhyssa persuasoria* using her antennae to scent out and find the larva of a horntail (see page 39), which tunnels along tree trunks. When she finds one, she uses her ovipositor as a drill to bore down to the larvae and place an egg on its body. It hatches and her larva then feeds on the body of the horntail larva. By sweeping your net among wild flowers, especially in damp habitats, you may find some of these wasps.

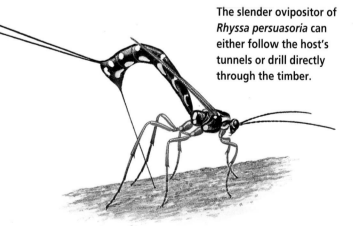

The slender ovipositor of *Rhyssa persuasoria* can either follow the host's tunnels or drill directly through the timber.

Order: Hymenoptera—Family: Ichneumonidae
U.S. & Canada species: 3,000
World species: 20,000
Body length: ⅛–2 in (0.3–5 cm)

Platygastrid Wasps

Most species of platygastrid wasps lay eggs in the eggs or very young larvae of gall midges (see page 77), mealy bugs, or whiteflies (see page 75, both). Species of *Inostemma* (shown here) have a forward-pointing "handle," which contains the ovipositor (egg-laying tube). Their habitats are widespread, but closely correspond to the presence of whatever may be their host species. The life history of many species of these very small, shiny, black insects is still unknown.

Order: Hymenoptera—Family: Platygastridae
U.S. & Canada species: 192—World species: 950
Body length:
¹⁄₁₆–⅛ in (0.15–0.3 cm)

Torymid Wasps

Because these wasps are very small, the best way to find them is to collect some galls and keep them until insects emerge (see page 65). You can tell these wasps from others that may also emerge, by their bright, shiny, metallic blue or green bodies. They will also have bent antennae and the ovipositor may be as long as, or even longer than, the rest of the body. While most species parasitize the occupants of galls, others parasitize caterpillars, and the larvae of solitary bees and wasps, and some lay their eggs in the seeds of conifers, hawthorns, and apple and pear trees.

Order: Hymenoptera—Family: Torymidae
U.S. & Canada species: 175—World species: 1,500
Body length: ¹⁄₁₆–½ in (0.15–1.3 cm)

Apple seed chalcid
(Torymus varians)

Scelionid Wasps

Like the platygastrid wasps, scelionid wasps have bent or elbowed antennae. Most of the adults are solitary and lay their eggs in the newly laid eggs of moths or butterflies. To be sure of such freshness, these wasps have evolved the habit of clinging to the host insect until she lays her eggs. Some even lose their wings once they have found and boarded a suitable host insect.

The species shown here, *Telenomus dalmanni*, parasitizes moth eggs.

Order: Hymenoptera
Family: Scelionidae
U.S. & Canada species: 275
World species: 1,250
Body length:
¹⁄₁₆–½ in (0.15–1.3 cm)

Trichogrammatid Wasps

These wasps lay their eggs into the eggs of a variety of other insects. To observe these tiny wasps, you will need to collect insect eggs and wait to see what emerges. It is possible that one of the emerging insects will be an undescribed species, because the habits of so many of these wasps are still unknown. The females of some species of this wasp swim underwater in search of the eggs of dragonflies and aquatic insects. Some species are very useful in controlling pest species.

Order: Hymenoptera
Family:
Trichogrammatidae
U.S. & Canada
species: 43

World species: 532
Body length:
¹⁄₃₂–¹⁄₁₆ in (0.8–1.6 mm)

Trichogramma semblidis

Pests & Parasites

Silverfish & Firebrats

You may see some of these small, wingless, grayish or silver-scaled insects running in the kitchen or bathroom at night. The rear end has three taillike filaments. These insects feed on flour, damp textiles, books, and wallpaper. Most species live outdoors, so look for them under stones, in debris, and in ants' nests—they run for cover very fast, which often saves their lives. The silverfish (*Lepisma saccarina*, shown here) prefers cool, damp places, while firebrats often stay near hot pipes and ovens.

Order: Thysanura—Family: Lepismatidae
U.S. & Canada species: 13
World species: 200
Body length:
⅓–¾ in (0.8–2 cm)

German Cockroaches

Members of this family look shiny and are generally brown or light brown in color. They have long, slender legs and long, thin antennae. Although they have wings, they seldom fly. A female lays an average of five egg cases in her lifetime, and each one may contain about 30 eggs. From each of these a young cockroach emerges, which looks exactly like a small adult. The German cockroach (*Blatella germanica*, shown here) counts as a major household pest. They have an unpleasant smell, which will be obvious to you if they are around.

Order: Blattaria
Family: Blattellidae
U.S. & Canada species: 24
World species: 1,750
Body length: ½ in
(1.3 cm)

Clothes Moths

You may find some species from this family around rotting wood and fungi in a variety of habitats, but they are most common indoors where their larvae feed on woolen fabrics. The female webbing clothes moth (*Tineola bisselliella*, shown here) lays about 100 eggs in the folds of clothing. When the larvae emerge, they spin a tube made from the gnawed material as a protection against drying out. With the increase of synthetic fibers and insect repellents, many of the family are becoming scarcer, though some remain serious pests, particularly in museums.

Order: Lepidoptera
Family: Tineidae
U.S. & Canada species: 180
World species: 2,500
Body length:
⅓–¾ in (0.8–2 cm)

Bed Bugs

These blood-sucking bugs have oval, flattened bodies, and some have a covering of silky hairs. They are parasitic on humans, other mammals, and birds. Where humans live in crowded and unsanitary places, bed bugs are common. At night they suck the blood of their hosts and return to their hiding places. In a single meal an adult bed bug (*Cimex lectularius*, shown here) can suck up seven times its own weight of blood. The nymphs take 6 to 26 weeks to develop—they need a blood meal at each of the five molts during their growth.

Order: Hemiptera
Family: Cimicidae
U.S. & Canada species: 14
World species: 90
Body length: ¼ in
(0.6 cm)

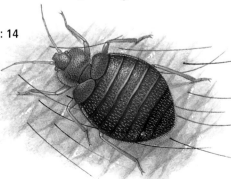

Wax & Tortoise Scale Insects

In general, scale insects are oval and flattened and have a hard waxy or smooth body. Most of the females remain fixed in one place on a plant and do not look like insects at all. Brown soft scale (*Coccus hesperidum,* shown here) is a pest of greenhouse crops and citrus trees. A single female may produce hundreds of millions of eggs in one year. From these emerge nymphs, called "crawlers," who move away from their mother before pushing their "beaks" into the plant to suck sap. Many nymphs produce wax filaments that allow them to lift off on the wind and travel great distances.

Order: Hemiptera—Family: Coccidae
U.S. & Canada species: 92
World species: 1,250
Body length: ¹⁄₁₆–½ in (0.15–1.3 cm)

Whiteflies

If you know someone who runs a commercial greenhouse, you may have heard about whiteflies. The females of the greenhouse whitefly (*Trialeurodes vaporariorum,* shown here) lay eggs on the underside of leaves of tomato and other plants. The nymphs suck the plant sap and excrete a sticky substance that promotes the growth of an unsightly mold on the plant or its fruit. A whitefly population explosion can be controlled by using a small parasitic wasp called *Encarsia formosa.* This is cheaper and safer than using chemicals.

Order: Hemiptera
Family: Aleyrodidae
U.S. & Canada species: 99
World species: 1,200
Body length: ¹⁄₁₀ in
(0.25 cm)

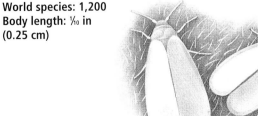

Mealy Bugs

Unlike other scale insects, members of this family have legs at all stages in their life cycle. The females are wingless and are covered in a mealy or waxy white coating. The males look more like regular insects with a pair of wings, but their mouthparts are undeveloped, so they cannot feed. All mealy bug species are sap suckers. The females of some species lay eggs, but others give birth to live nymphs. Mealy bugs are found on a variety of host plants; each species tends to keep to a particular type of plant.

Order: Hemiptera
Family: Pseudococcidae
U.S. & Canada species: 280
World species: 2,000
Body length: ¹⁄₁₆–¹⁄₈ in
(0.15–0.3 cm)

 Pseudococcus adonidum

Leaf-footed Bugs

The males of some species have strong hind legs armed with spines. These are used in territorial fighting for access to females. All species are herbivorous (plant-eating) and defend themselves by spraying a pungent, unpleasant fluid at their enemies. Some species may be found feeding on St.-John's-wort, grasses, and other plants. In North America, a few species damage members of the gourd family—including melons, marrows, and pumpkins.

Order: Hemiptera
Family: Coreidae
U.S. & Canada species: 120
World species: 2,000
Body length: ⅓–1½ in
(0.8–3.8 cm)

Coriomeris scabricornis

Dermestid Beetles

This family of small beetles can be found in a huge variety of indoor and outdoor habitats. They are also known as skin, larder, and museum beetles. The larvae eat mainly the dried remains of plants or animals, including hair and feathers. Others thrive on a diet of carpets, fur, spices, or dried milk. Many museum collections of organic (plant- or animal-based) materials have been destroyed by the varied carpet beetle (*Anthrenus verbasci*, shown here). The adults mostly eat pollen from flowers.

Order: Coleoptera—Family: Dermestidae
U.S. & Canada species: 129
World species: 800
Body length: ⅟₁₆–½ in (0.15–1.3 cm)

Scarab Beetles

The sacred scarabs of ancient Egypt are part of this family. Their habitat is extremely varied, but includes fungi, flowers, dung, bark, and the nests of ants, termites, and vertebrates. There are many sub-families with common names like dung beetles, cockchafers, skin beetles, rose chafers, rhinoceros, and Hercules beetles. It is one of the largest families of beetles with 1,400 species. In early summer, you may see and hear a Junebug, a type of scarab, flying toward a lighted window on a warm night.

Order: Coleoptera
Family: Scarabaeidae
U.S. & Canada species: 1,400
World species: 20,000
Body length: ⅟₁₆–6 in (0.15–15 cm)

Serica brunnea

Pea & Bean Weevils

These pests of stored products lay their eggs on seeds and these produce whitish, grublike larvae that burrow into peas and beans. Many larvae may develop inside a single seed, destroying it. When fully grown, they pupate near the surface of the seed and on emergence they chew their way out. This action leaves a small, round hole—a sure sign that the culprit was a pea or bean weevil. Some species attack crops in the field, like the cowpea weevil (*Callosobruchus maculatus*, shown here).

Order: Coleoptera
Family: Bruchidae
U.S. & Canada species: 135
World species: 1,300
Body length: ⅟₁₆–¾ in (0.15–2 cm)

Click Beetles

These beetles have the ability to click loudly and throw themselves into the air when lying on their backs. The very loud click and the sudden movement will frighten any predator, while moving the beetle out of harm's way. They are also found on oak trees and the ground under leaf litter and in decaying wood. The larvae are called wireworms because they are thin and tough-bodied. They are found under bark, in rotten wood, and in soil.

Order: Coleoptera
Family: Elateridae
U.S. & Canada species: 700
World species: 8,000
Body length: ⅟₁₆–2⅓ in (0.15–3.3 cm)

Lined click beetle
(*Agriotes lineatus*)

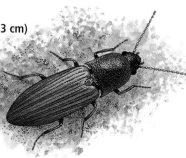

Gall Midges

Many members of this family lay eggs in the leaves of such plants as daisy, grass, and willow and so cause galls to form. They can be found anywhere that their host plants grow. Some species of gall midges produce larvae that are parasitic on small insect mites, while others are predators. A few species live in fungi, and some even live in galls made by other insects.

The larva of the Hessian fly (Mayetiola destructor) is a pest on wheat.

Order: Diptera—Family: Cecidomyiidae
U.S. & Canada species: 1,060
World species: 4,600
Body length: ¹⁄₁₆–⅓ in (0.15–0.8 cm)

Pomace Flies

Tiny flies of this family, also known as vinegar flies (*Drosophila melanogaster*), have been studied in more detail than any other animal. *Drosophila melanogaster* are of help in the study of heredity because they can be easily bred on artificial foods and reproduce very fast. In the wild they are found near rotting fruit, and elsewhere in food and drink processing factories. Search around decaying fallen apples to find tiny flies with red eyes that look like the *Drosophila funebris* shown here.

Order: Diptera
Family: Drosophilidae
U.S. & Canada species: 117
World species: 2,900
Body length: ¹⁄₁₆–¼ in (0.15–0.6 cm)

Clear-winged Moths

These moths are truly amazing. They mimic social wasps, bees, or ichneumon wasps (see page 72), and resemble them very closely in body shape and color. Even their wings are almost free of scales. The hornet moth (*Sesia apiformis*, shown here) mimics a hornet. They complete the mimicry by buzzing, and some species even pretend to sting, so if you do see one, look carefully and make sure it really is a clear-winged moth. They can be seen around flowers in a variety of habitats.

Order: Lepidoptera
Family: Sesiidae
U.S. & Canada species: 120
World species: 1,000
Body length: ½–1½ in (1.3–3.8 cm)

Gelechiid Moths

These small to tiny moths form one of the largest moth families. The caterpillars of some species protect themselves by rolling leaves into a tube fastened with their silk. Others spin shelters of silk in the leaves, shoots, or flower heads of host plants. By looking closely at a number of oak leaves in late summer, you should be able to find some of these leaf-rollers. Many species are pests on crops, such as potatoes, tomatoes, strawberries, and soft fruit and cotton.

Order: Lepidoptera
Family: Gelechiidae
U.S. & Canada species: 635
World species: 4,200
Body length: ¼–1 in (0.6–2.5 cm)

Metzneria lappella

Find Out More

Glossary

abdomen: third section of an insect's body; it carries the ovipositor and the stinger, if any

carnivore: any animal that eats mostly meat

ecosystem: interactions of plants and animals that form a living habitat

ectoparasite: harmful, parasitic organism that lives on the surface of an animal's body

endoparasite: harmful, parasitic organism that lives inside an animal's body

enzymes: substances produced by the body to speed up chemical reactions (for example, to help digest food)

gall: growth produced by a plant around the eggs of gall wasps and gnats

habitat: environment (area) that is the natural home of certain plants and animals

herbivore: any animal that eats mostly plants

honeydew: sweet substance produced by aphids and other tiny insects

insectivore: animal, such as a shrew, that eats mostly insects

invertebrate: animal without an internal backbone

larva: a young stage in the development of certain insects, which looks very different than the adult stage (for example, a caterpillar that later becomes a butterfly)

microhabitat: small area, such as a compost heap or window box, in which an animal lives

nectar: sugary liquid produced by flowering plants and eaten by insects and birds

nymph: young stage of certain winged insects, such as grasshoppers; nymphs may look much like the adult stage

omnivore: any animal that eats both plants and animals

ovipositor: egg-laying structure on the abdomen of an adult female insect; in some insects, the ovipositor also acts as a stinger

pheromone: chemical substance produced by insects (and certain other animals) that affects the behavior or development of other members of their species

proboscis: tubular, sucking mouthpiece of certain insects

pupa: inactive stage of an insect when it changes from a wingless larva to a winged adult

queen: a fully developed female in a colony of insects, such as bees or ants, that lays eggs

rostrum: beaklike extension at the front of the head of some insects, such as weevils

secretion: substance produced by a gland in the body, often containing enzymes

thorax: middle section of an insect's body. It is divided into three segments, each of which carries a pair of legs; the back two segments of the thorax also support the wings, if the insect has any

tymbals: drumlike organs on either side of the thorax of a cicada; they vibrate to make the insect's song

viviparous: giving birth to live young, instead of laying eggs

Organizations

The **American Entomological Society** is for professional entomologists and serious amateurs. The group publishes *Entomological News*. Contact: American Entomological Society, Academy of Natural Sciences of Philadelphia, 1900 Benjamin Franklin Parkway, Philadelphia, Pennsylvania 19103-1028; (215) 561-3978. http://www.acnatsci.org/hosted/aes/index.html

The Dragonfly Society of the Americas focuses on these spectacular insects. Write to: The Dragonfly Society of the Americas, 2067 Little River Lane, Tallahassee, Florida 32311. http://www.afn.org/~iori/dsaintro.html

The Lepidopterists' Society publishes a journal and a newsletter. Write to: The Lepidopterists' Society, 9417 Carvalho Court, Bakersfield, California 93311-1846. http://alpha.furman.edu/~snyder/snyder/lep/index1.htm

The **Xerces Society** is a national society for invertebrate (animals without backbones) enthusiasts. Contact: Xerces Society, 4828 SE Hawthorne Boulevard, Portland, Oregon 97215; (503) 232-6639. http://www.xerces.org

The **Young Entomologists' Society** publishes a magazine containing articles about insects that are of interest to the beginner. Write to: Young Entomologists' Society, 6907 West Grand River Avenue, Lansing, Michigan 48906-9131. http://members.aol.com/YESbugs/mainmenu.html

Index

Additional Resources

Bugs: A Close-Up View of the Insect World
Christopher Maynard (Dorling Kindersley, 2001).

***Bugs A–Z: An A to Z of Insects and Creepy
Crawlies*** Jill Bailey (Blackbirch Press, 2002).

Classifying Insects Andrew Solway (Heinemann
Library, 2003).

***The Insect Book: A Basic Guide to the Collection
and Care of Common Insects for Children***
Connie Zakowski (Rainbow Books, 1997).

Insectlopedia Douglas Florian (Harcourt, 1998).

Insects L. A. Mound (Dorling Kindersley, 2003).

Insects and Spiders Edward Parker (Raintree
Steck-Vaughn, 2003).

The Life Cycle of Insects Louise and Richard
Spilsbury (Heinemann Library, 2003).

Index